Living Dhaka, Leaving Dhaka
Memories of Bangladesh

By Mehnaaz Momen

জাগৃতি প্রকাশনী

Living Dhaka, Leaving Dhaka
By Mehnaaz Momen

First Edition   : February 2022

Published by   : Razia Rahman
Jagriti Prokashony, Office 107 (Ground floor)
Concord Emporium, Kataban 253, 254
Elephant Road Dhaka-1205 & 38/4
Banglabazar, 1st floor, Dhaka-1100

Cover   : Dhruba Esh

Decoration   : Shamim Ahmed

Printing   : Frontview, 261/3, Fokirapool
Motijheel, Dhaka-1000

Price   : BDT 400 or USD ....

ISBN   : 978-984-96262-1-3

To buy online
www.rokomari.com, jagritiprokashony

Acknowledgements

This memoir is a personal narration of coming of age for a particular generation of girls in Dhaka. Without enthusiastic support from the characters of the story, this book would have been incomplete. My family members, especially my sister Nausheen, and my friends Miti, Moniza and Laila, were eager readers from the very beginning, often reminding me of incidents I had overlooked. My friends from the university quarters and Udayan Bidyalaya helped me out with pictures that captured the essence of the bygone era. Laila Nahar was the only photographer in my circle of close friends and it is her pictures—except for the family pictures—that adorn this book. She donated her time and technical expertise to restore the old and shabby images to convey the aura of a period that fostered Dhaka girls into womanhood.

Contents

Prologue

Twenty years ago, in ill-fitted jeans and a jacket that was too big and warm for August, with two huge suitcases and an odd-shaped carry-on without any wheels, I boarded a British Airways flight to New York, with the ultimate goal of landing in Halifax, Nova Scotia. I was about to start my master's program at Dalhousie University, an exciting and scary detour back into the academic world after working in Bangladesh for two years. I was leaving behind my childhood, my adolescence, and my early youth along with my parents, my husband of three years, and my lifelong memories.

I can see myself dressed in my newly bought jeans from Bangabazar, the marketplace for redundant garments that did not make it to the import quota, usually for a trivial flaw; the kameez, long enough to be considered part of traditional attire, yet hip enough for a top (or so I hoped); and the jacket that I really did not need in mid-August, neither in Dhaka, nor in New York, my first stop to meet my uncles and my sister.

My family in Dhaka bade me goodbye, my mom saying with teary eyes, "Take care of yourself"; my dad saying with excitement, "I think you've chosen a good program"; my in-laws saying dejectedly, "Come back safely and soon"; and my husband, holding my hand and queasy about the effect on our marriage, telling me, "What if I don't get to see you again, ever?"

At Heathrow Airport I tagged along my heavy grim blue carry-on which would not fit in the restroom and which I dared not leave without supervision. I had been warned that leaving one's bag even for a minute was dangerous as drug traffickers lurked around to find unsuspecting pieces of baggage in which to smuggle their drugs. I could not identify anyone with dangerous motives, but was unable to sleep and decided to have a cup of tea.

The cup of tea, which I had taken for granted every morning at home, at street junctures, or anywhere at any time in Dhaka, posed a set of problems at Heathrow. I needed cash and I needed it in British currency. I changed my precious twenty-dollar bill into pounds and went back to the tea shop. While the girl at the counter waited with a look of impatience until I could figure out the exact change, and while I tried to hurry up, more than a little flustered, a tall lean man came to my rescue, saying, "I got it," and putting his large palm over the sea of coins that my two hands could barely contain. Both the girl at the counter and I heaved a sigh of relief. I can still see his towering angular body, slightly bent toward me, and the reddish brown bushy moustache. His small act of kindness almost smoothed the sharp edges of a lifelong history lesson, the two hundred years of British colonial history, the excruciatingly long process of getting American and Canadian visas while standing outside in the sun and rain for hours, and the callous indifference of the embassy staff. Meanwhile, the tea was insipid and adding cream and sugar only subtracted the little flavor that was left. The first thing I missed from home was a strong cup of tea.

The next seven years in Halifax, Canada, and Cleveland, Ohio constituted my long sojourn as a graduate and PhD student. Talking to my sister Nausheen and my childhood friend Moniza was often the only respite from the stress-filled life I was enduring, the divorce I was trying to recover from, and the confusion and ambiguity of the new life I had landed in. For years I spent a lion's share of my meager scholarship money talking to Nausheen and Moniza over the phone, sometimes to laugh, sometimes to vent the nagging feeling of not belonging, sometimes to analyze relationships, especially my failed marriage. The countless hours of analyzing love, life, and pain guided me through the maze of cultural confusion, the initial immigrant plights. Yet there was something additional brewing in our exchanges, something that contained more than the three of us or our friends and cohorts, but was rather a piece of Bangladesh, or at least urban middle-class Dhaka, the space which was in transition when we were growing up, shaping us and allowing us to grow and change along with it.

We grew up in the seventies, in the aftermath of our Liberation War, when the shackles of religious and cultural mores relaxed for a decade, the U.S. and the Soviet Union fought to win our hearts and minds during the Cold War, and a porous new world opened up where it was possible and even commonplace to question everything from religion to politics to identity. We grew up listening to, participating in, and mired in confusion over the debates involving capitalism versus socialism, Islam versus Westernization, and Bengali versus Bangladeshi.

America in the nineties welcomed us with open arms, making it possible for the first time to travel by ourselves as we wished, granting control over our lives that we never had as girls growing up in a traditional society. We made frequent travel plans, me often via Greyhound to meet up with old friends scattered all over America in graduate programs. We relished these get-togethers, nostalgic to the hilt, trying to figure out who we were becoming. Like an artist viewing the splash of colors in her own unfinished project I became interested in my scattered thoughts and tattered memories and saw that the colors and shape of the painting looked different depending on the distance. Maybe the seeds of this story started germinating then, though I was oblivious to it.

As a graduate assistant I assisted my professor Sanda Kaufman in interviews and analysis of a local community project and we shared stories, hers from Romania and Israel, mine from Bangladesh. She was dumbfounded when I recalled Clever Masha and other Russian stories I grew up reading, the same ones she had read in Romania. Any queries about religion and culture had special significance since she grew up in Israel in her teenage years and had quite different perceptions of Islam. I grappled with the distance between my lived experiences and the cultural lenses available to shed light on different practices. One of my aunts never prayed, but dutifully put on the burqa or Islamic covering to signal her status as the union chairman's wife in the village. Example after example flashed through my mind during discussions of religion, Islam, terrorism, and the subjugation of women, most conflicting with the official storyline or subverting the dominant view.

Later at my teaching job in Laredo, Texas, my sociologist friend Phoebe and anthropologist friend Jackie were not only curious about my past, but demanded explanations of the contradictions and ironies in my cultural makeup. How to explain my discomfort over assigning gender to God, which I am forced to do when I speak and think in English? My language, Bengali, does not contain gender variation, which allowed me to imagine a God without gender specification. Stripped of a human persona, God forever remained distant to me, only to be approached before an examination or some other crisis. But the God, both Islamic and Christian, that was being discussed in Laredo, and in post-9/11 America, had too many human traits and was too interfering with both wrath and love. Teaching as I did in a border city on the Texas/Mexico border, I saw manifestations of the culture of poverty, such as the effort to transform everything growing in nature—like cactus—into something edible, just as we in Bangladesh used to cook the skins of various vegetables rather than throwing them away. Instead of becoming scared by cars being driven dangerously close to each other, I felt more at home. I laughed at the practice of not honking but sticking the head out of the car and screaming at someone. The lack of personal space and the norm of asking questions of strangers, say in line at the grocery store, made me smile and enjoy the experience, the very thing that irritated me to no end back home. This was the one place in America where I looked like most people, yet did not understand the language.

The patriotic fervor of the post-9/11 world also caused me to pause and take a hard look at myself. As I was critiquing the decimation of civil liberties, the high-handedness of the government, and the drowning of reason amid the chanting of patriotic slogans, I realized that I myself grew up in a time right after liberation when school started with the national anthem and most of the television programs were driven by patriotic messages. My friends and I, in fact almost everyone I can think of, passionately debated politics, both domestic and international, because both America and the Soviet Union were trying to get us into their respective camps in the Cold War era. At the same time, we were quite oblivious to the plight of our own minorities, especially the small tribal minorities like the Chakma, the Garo, and the Monipuri people who resided in the hilly regions with their colorful clothes and spectacular dance rituals. They remained outside our consciousness despite regime after regime violating their rights, even as we kept arguing about the abstractions of capitalism versus socialism at local tea stalls. I had grown up considering patriotism an essential part of one's character, but now I was witnessing the ugly side of it. As I was looking at American society critically and trying to understand the nature and logic of the disturbing trends that were setting in, I could not help but analyze my own cultural composition which prioritized patriotism and Bengali identity. The eternal conflict between being a Muslim or a Bengali always came into play, whether it was over choosing names for children (Arabic/Persian or Bengali), deciding to wear the tip on the forehead (identifying with Bengali/Hindu culture), or figuring out whether to support India or Pakistan in cricket matches (still a major indicator of the dominance of Bengali versus Muslim identity).

My friends and I enjoyed a more privileged upbringing compared to the rest of our cohorts who lived in non-urban and poorer households, though we lacked what would today be considered basic freedoms and access to entertainment. The soft cultural taboo against dating tinged romantic relationships with such hues that no real relationship could keep up with our expectations. With all our cultural training to be "good girls" and "good wives," we were thoroughly unprepared for the ups and downs of real relationships. My own six-year-long romantic odyssey—which began with fighting against all odds, then getting married, and then experiencing the final meltdown and divorce within a few years—left me stunned and prone to reconsider everything I had learned and the advice from all directions that was continually being bestowed upon me.

In more ways than one, my coming of age mirrored the transition of Dhaka itself. Post-liberation Bangladesh in the seventies opened up a space for ambiguity, clashes, resistance, and friction between old and new, love and desperation, familiarity and strangeness. Rising from the ashes of war—wounded, uncertain, triumphant—Dhaka was growing awkwardly with its shiny buildings and bustling street corners. We resided in the cultural hub of the city, basking in innocence, friendship, and romance, and yearning for more freedom to claim the city each day. Witnessing each other's transition from adolescence to youth, watching each other's dreams that were being born, crushed, and renewed en route, my city and I came of age in the promising seventies as well as the turbulent eighties.

Back in Cleveland during my student days, I used to read Counterpunch, one of the few online political websites which dared to criticize Bush administration policies and civil rights violations in 2001, before it became acceptable and fashionable to do so later on. I was looking for a book by one of their authors, and, on a whim, sent off an email asking about his publications. He surprised me by responding to it and we started conversing, and then when we met I became witness to and part of the struggles of an aspiring writer. Having spent his formative years in California, his political sensibilities toward both America and the Indian subcontinent (his parents were migrants to Pakistan from Gujarat after 1947) were very different than mine. When we were not arguing passionately to defend our different positions, he wanted to know my story. He had just enough political and cultural knowledge about my background to be curious, but not enough not to get surprised. As the most attentive and curious listener of my stories, he nudged my recollections toward a shape which was hazy at first, though I could begin to see the silhouette of a picture I had buried somewhere deep within me. This is how the book started in slow halting steps, but its steady pace took me to places I had forgotten or never appreciated in full.

So I conjure my own looking glass to ponder my childhood, my adolescence, my marriage and divorce, and my reflections about the days after coming over to America. My computer screen turns into a magic mirror, where my life flashes by, catching me off guard, at once connecting and distancing me from the life that I left behind. As I dissect myself in the world which was part of me as I was part of it, I acknowledge my debt for the privileges that I enjoyed and that my country could ill-afford at the time. The bittersweet taste of that world lingers on as I try to fathom the piercing agony, mesmerizing beauty, and unending confusion of strange words—angular, linear—demanding explanations yet pushing me to be scrupulous enough to press on to unravel uncomfortable truths and appreciate the raw splendor of vibrance and irony.

How can I not chronicle this journey which overlaps with that of so many of my friends, taking us back to what we left behind, shining a light on the lazy afternoons with a guava in one hand and a storybook in another, the rain-filled days, the aimless walks in the scorching sun, the starry nights—none of which are lost, but live on quietly and stubbornly?

People

The smell of wet earth. The sticky soil filled with dead and dried flowers. The emerald green of leaves washed by the rain. The moist cool air. The splendor of the yellow and white of the trees in winter, not the bright red, orange, and lilac of summer. The warmth of the sun after the morning mist.

The most uncomplicated of my memories are those winter mornings in Kuliarchar, my ancestral village, an unremarkable little rural area with a couple of schools and colleges and a cold storage industry to freeze and market fish, less than a hundred miles from Dhaka. Winter is dry in Bangladesh, but I remember the short showers that didn't drench you but only created a lot of diversion. Even the tiniest drops set off a great deal of noise: "Close the window," "Get the clothes from the balcony," "Cover the food that is being dried in the sun," "Winter rain, it brings the cold wave," or "Winter rain is such a tease, don't panic, it will be over in a few minutes."

After causing so much commotion it was over, leaving behind a pleasing touch that dampened the chilly air and made everything clean and bright. We, the urban visitors to our ancestral village, sat outside on the open balcony, looking at the small pond, the huge badam tree, and the green fields which ended at the riverbank. The passersby walking on the narrow makeshift path along the pond stopped and talked to us while we sat in the sun, taking in all the warmth the weak rays could offer. We tried to boost the warmth with a cup of hot tea, always too sweet. My dada, or paternal grandfather, asked, "What is going on with the country?" and my dad responded with his dramatized pessimistic view of politics, "There is nothing good stored in the future for us, everything is going backwards," until breakfast was served: chhiter ruti, flatbread made of rice flour, which looked like a spider's web, crunchy and airy in the mouth; and the spread of the yellow of scrambled eggs, the almost red of last night's leftover chicken, and the green of the morning's quickly concocted dish against the white ruti. The fluffy crispness melted in the mouth against the zest and spices that lingered on.

The food was cooked by Bini and her mother who worked for my dada, and they were as permanent as the brick bungalow with its tin roof standing awkwardly among the bamboo houses. Bini was younger than my mom; dark, with her curly hair peeking from under her head covered with the saree, she was forever smiling and quickly surprised. Her mother, who always seemed too old, was the only one who had seen my dadi, my grandmother, who died young, so we often asked her to share her memories. The description she used over and over about my dadi was, "She had compassion [maya] in her heart."

The dark kitchen was outside the house, as was customary in villages, surrounded by bamboo walls and the mud stove that was lighted with wood and bamboo splinters. My sister and I begged Bini to let us blow into the fire of the stove. The dimple on her dark face lighting up with a smile and the nose pin glistening in the fire of the stove, Bini obliged, telling us to be careful. The kitchen was always warm and stuffy with smoke, wonderful in winter and dreadful in summer. At night, the sharp flames from kupi, the kerosene-lighted lamp, and the hazier ones from the glass domes of the hariken, the larger lamp, along with the constant fire of the stove created the unearthly feeling of a cave separated from civilization. The main house was only ten steps away; we jumped over the bricks between the house and the kitchen during the day, but at night carefully placed our feet on the bricks to take us back to the safety inside the concrete walls of the bungalow, under its noisy tin roof and its offering of a little more light that produced enormous shadows on the wall.

The journey to Kuliarchar, our village, was an adventure in itself, one that we did not look forward to. The trains were invariably late—if we were lucky, only by a couple of hours. The compartments were so overcrowded that we could barely make out the slim hard benches where women and children were piled up. It was harder for men to get a place to sit as chivalry was expected of them with the utterance, "Brother—women and children, women and children first!" A number of people crouched on the ground, usually without a ticket, disappearing when the ticket collector, or TT, was about to arrive, and coming back from nowhere as soon as the train started to move. Two stations prior to Kuliarchar we needed to change the train in Bhairab, the main junction in Mymensingh, and board a train toward Chittagong, which was even more overcrowded. We got the Issa Khan Express, the direct train which took about five to six hours in the late seventies; now it takes less than three hours to drive from Dhaka to our village home.

The excitement of the journey, getting up early, and packing and hurrying soon gave way to infinite boredom within a day at

Kuliarchar. Either my sister, Nausheen, or I asked my mom, "What do we do now?" and the silent anger and irritation in my mother's eyes sufficed as an answer. There were the long lazy days with nothing to do, no one to play or speak with, less than a hundred miles from Dhaka but a million miles away from civilization. There was no television, only a battery-powered radio blasting advertisements peppered with songs and dramas which we liked, but in our home the radio was on only every couple of hours for the news. Electricity came a few years later, but only after sunset, and so weak that the bulbs were dimmer than hariken, the small lantern that ran on kerosene and could be carried anywhere as a personal light.

Walking along the railway track, or rail line as we called it, and collecting oval gray and bluish pebbles, was a cherished ritual as soon as we started walking toward our half-brick tin-roofed bungalow, nestled among the half-mud houses. The first thing I saw outside after moving the bamboo partition was the tubewell, then the kitchen, removed from the main house and made of bamboo walls. Before entering the main house, I often sneaked into the storage room, another structure opposite the kitchen, where patkhori (a very light stick made from jute) was stored for lighting the stove; it made a wonderful crunchy sound when I broke it. I won't deny that my heart beat even faster coming back to Dhaka during the scooter ride from the Kamalapur station to our house (an apartment really) in the university area in anticipation of catching up with my friends and missed television shows.

Often it was a challenge to get inside our house as my dad with his lifelong fear of theft burglar-proofed our house in such a way that even we could not go back in after an exhausting journey.

My mom never trusted his tactics, arguing, "Please, let's not miss the train to derail the thieves!" Once he put part of a razor blade inside the lock when we all went to Kuliarchar for Eid to make it a challenge for a thief to break in. No thieves attempted entry, but my dad cut his finger trying to get the razor blade out of the lock.

Aspiring boys often left the village to go to school, then to work, and finally to settle in the city. Lucky girls were married off to grooms in Dhaka or other cities. Everyone moved to the city, but kept coming back to bari, a word used for home, never applied to the one in the city. The word for the house, not home, in the city was basha. If one was asked where was your bari, the question was about where you were from; if one was asked where was your basha, the question was about where you lived. Unless we coordinated our visit with cousins, which happened once or twice a year during Eid or the summer holidays, the trip to my village home was lonely. I bargained with my mom over how many books I could take because we didn't want to make the luggage too heavy while we changed trains and fought for seats for the long five to eight hour journey (depending on the lateness of the train) to a place so near, yet so far. I always had fewer books than I needed. Often I closed my eyes and tried to imagine an alternative ending to the story I had just read.

We looked forward to playing with Bokul and Putul, Bini's daughters. Even though Bokul was my age, being the maid's daughter she had lost her playing privileges earlier than me and I had to be satisfied with the younger Putul. Bokul was dark with curly hair and had a sweet smile like her mother, but Putul was fair, petite, and lithe. I remember how both of their nose pins glittered in the sun when we ran and in the light of the lamps at night. Soon it was inappropriate for me to play as well. Little girls grow up too quickly in Bangladesh, especially in the villages. The games were simple hide-and-seek, hopscotch, or running to the riverbank. "Are the pictures lifelike on television?" or "Is the electric light as bright as the sun?" were the two sisters' typical queries when the village was still a galaxy away from Dhaka.

Bini, along with her younger sister Lily, and their mom, were a stable part of our household—these were the women who had children but no husband. Abandoning wives and little children was quite common in Bangladesh and there was no social safety net other than a father or a brother willing to bear the financial burden. Women working as maids in both rural and urban areas shared the same pathetic story of husbands leaving them behind. I wonder about their love life now. Contrary to common perceptions about traditional culture, romance was not absent but rather short-lived under the onerous practical concerns. The abundance of children attested to the prevalence of sexual relations; sex was perhaps the only recreation available to the poor for free. Tolerance for extramarital affairs and out of wedlock children was much higher in rural societies back in the seventies before religion became the prime thread of the social narrative. Bini's husband was long gone when she had her younger daughter Putul, but Bini never uttered a word about Putul's father and was allowed her privacy, which seems inconceivable today as fatwas, or religious edicts, regarding extramarital relations are common in villages. Fatwas started slowly germinating in the eighties with regard to immoral conduct and continue to threaten not only the freedom and well-being of the one on trial (always the woman, even if she is the rape victim), but also the authority of the judicial system itself.

Bini's sister Lily was supple and graceful, and had a strong yet pleasant personality that did not match her illiterate upbringing. After a couple of failed relationships with men who were above her social status, she finally got married but her husband promptly disappeared when she got pregnant. The last she heard of him was that he was in a jail in Pakistan for smuggling girls. Lily was far too energetic and intelligent for her peers. She never went to school yet could discuss politics—local, national, or even international—with ease, and though she could barely read, her advice and recommendations were eagerly sought by my dad and uncles when it came to issues of land—whom to lease to, where to sell. She has survived her whole life on the meager salary doled out by my dad and uncles; chronic illness and repeated surgeries have failed to dampen her fiery spirit. Her son Pavel has turned out to be an impressive young man who is doing his bachelor's in economics at a college in Bhairab. He may not be going to a very reputable college, and his degree may not procure him a strictly white-collar position, but his going to college itself is a cause for celebration. The impact of cultural change for his family is not negligible. Pavel may well attain the opportunities his hard-working mother so richly deserved but never had. Regardless of the kind of job Pavel lands into, his education, his exposure to the world, and his cultural affiliation to class have changed dramatically from the generation before.

Bokul, my playmate, now a married mother of four daughters—the eldest working at a garment factory—is burdened with poverty; her sister Putul lives in nearby Bhairab, her four children are going to school, and she is in a not so happy situation with her husband who has another love interest. Instead of the usual lamentations over her fate, which was the norm in her mother's generation, she eagerly talks about her children, her pretty face shining with excitement. At her age, her mother looked and behaved like an old woman. Putul's most impressive accomplishment, however, is Nabila, her fifteen-year-old daughter studying in class nine, full of energy and spirit. Not only did she secure all As and only one B in her class eight shomaponi exam (the board exam), but she is also interested in books, music, and movies and is able to express herself clearly and articulately. I don't know the words to capture this sea change in the rural landscape, where young girls are not only going to school but growing up with exposure to the broader world and eager to explore their place in that world.

The house that dada designed as a bungalow with care—where Lily and Pavel live as caretakers and keep one room locked for dada's grandchildren to visit once in a while—feels empty and forlorn now. It seems like another lifetime when dada slowly walked toward the sunlight at mid-morning and sat in a chair on the balcony, slightly hunched, in his lungi and a white undershirt under his shawl, and asked me, "Can you spell mathematics?" My dad would look at me with a confident smile and my mom with doubt and apprehension. Dada said "good" or "correct" to the right answers, and remained silent if the answers were wrong, which was enough to dissolve us in shame. Thin and frail, he never lost much of his hair until the very end though he did lose his teeth and grew thinner with time. The next phase of my test was in the afternoon, when, after intensely studying the newspaper for hours, he called out to me, "Mehnaaz, let's see if you can translate this paragraph into English for me." The last phase was writing a letter, which he narrated in very formal language, sometimes to an uncle or aunt, sometimes a letter to the editor, as I carefully labored over the spelling in my best penmanship. I miss the presence of letters in my life, which I wrote and received with so much anticipation until what seems to have been only the other day, but was actually more than two decades ago.

The gap between the two yearly visits to Kuliarchar was filled with the exchange of letters. I was always at a loss as to what to write to dada. My life, my friends, my reading—I didn't find any of that appropriate to share. As for the news I really wanted— about the goats, the pond, the oparajita jhar (a blue flower that looks like the iris but grows in bushes, not on stems)—I didn't know how to articulate those queries. The letters were forced and formal, containing the status of my studies and inquiries about his health, such as, "Don't forget to take your cough medication. I stood second in the class. I got above eighty in all subjects except for geography and sports. Nausheen got ninety-five in math." I remember well the beige postcard with one and a half spaces (the other half reserved for writing the address), my mom assigning the full space to me (a privilege of the older sister) and the half to my sister. My dad didn't let me keep any space empty, saying, "We have paid for the whole space already!" Over the years, my letters became fewer and fewer, finally giving way to the few added lines to my mom's long letter, which she wrote religiously with zest. My mother can write page after page about nothing. I miss her letters that I got in Halifax and Cleveland, before I introduced her to the world of email, Facebook, and Skype.

Dada also baffled me with questions such as "How many miles is Runa's [my cousin's] house from yours?" I had no idea about the distance in miles as I calculated the distance in time. I answered, "It takes half an hour in a rickshaw," but he insisted on knowing the distance in miles, prodding me with, "How long would it take for you to walk there?" confusing me even more. Much later in urban studies classes, I figured out that measurement in time versus space is a classic urban/rural division and was his way of getting a feel for the place. He asked me what kind of trees I had seen around a particular place, which forced me to notice such things so as to be able to relate it to dada. I was in the second year of my bachelor's program when he died in 1988. With his death I lost my only connection to the slow pace of rural life.

I only saw him as the retired deputy magistrate who led a lonely life, as his wife had died in her late thirties, leaving him with six children (three of them under the age of ten). His decision not to marry again was unusual for his time. His job took him to new districts every year and my father and his siblings had to attend new schools each year. Dada was so tired of filling out the forms for the schools with such frequency that one year he put April 1 as the birthday for all of his children. This was not meant as an April Fool's joke, it was just the day he was filling out the form. As a result my dad and his brothers and sister all have April 1 as their birthday on their official matriculation certificates (since there was no provision for birth certificates, the first official certificate when one passed the nationwide exam after the tenth grade was considered the authoritative documentation on age).

I remember dada reclining on his low single bed, reading the newspaper or listening to the news on the radio. He prayed only once in the evening, the maghrib prayer, and the Friday noon or jumma prayer. As far as I remember, he only fasted on the twenty-seventh of Ramazan (the most auspicious day in the Islamic calendar), just like children did. I am curious about the meaning of these partial rituals, which were not half-hearted yet performed more as symbolic gestures than serious endeavors. I wonder where he would fit in post-9/11 perceptions of the mutually exclusive categories of practicing and non-practicing Muslims. I wish I knew what he believed in, but it never occurred to me to ask him such questions.

Nausheen brought out his fun-loving side, which he rarely showed. I can still see her taking care of the goat selected for her akika, the name-giving ceremony, and chasing the other small goats, babies really, with shining jet-black coats and springy sprints, running around in her pudgy feet, her straight hair all over her face. She was almost seven instead of the usual first year of life for the ceremony and stunned everyone by obstinately choosing a pet name (which rhymed with her best friend's name at the time) for herself. At first, everyone laughed at her request, but had to give in to her tears. My dada got a kick out of the episode and kept teasing my sister, "You have named yourself! How unique!" which she took as a compliment. Indeed, this was no small feat in a culture which strove to predetermine almost everything, especially for a girl.

The absence of my dadi, my grandmother, who had died too early, leaving behind my ten-year-old dad, lingered on in the dusty furniture, in the few treasured china dishes, in the way my dad became silent and evaded all questions about her. At the time of her death, her six children ranged from a married teenaged daughter to a five-year-old. My dad was very attached to her, a middle child engrossed in his studies with few friends and no aptitude for sports. On her deathbed, dadi had asked my chhoto phupu (youngest aunt) to comfort her with a handheld fan and being a five-year-old she stopped every once in a while, only to be reminded of her duty. "I wish I had stayed up all night and fanned her," she always added when she recounted her last memory of her mother. My chhoto chacha (youngest uncle) was the naughtiest and told me he wished he could take back all the incidents which had caused helpless sighs from dadi. Dadi's sisters, who were very young when dadi got married, also had stories about her quiet and diligent demeanor. Even though her father had been the education minister of undivided Bengal, she was humble and pleasing to everyone. She practiced homeopathy and I wish I knew how she learnt it in a time when she was not even allowed to go to school. She was taught to learn to read and write at home and I wonder why she had been interested in medicine. Was it the untimely death of her own mother?

Dadi took a long luxurious bath in the cold water from the earthen pitcher one summer day after she had been bedridden for several days due to an asthma attack and caught double pneumonia from which she never recovered. Once, my dada told us how happy she was when he brought back a bunch of sarees for her from Kolkata. He had tears in his eyes as he recollected, "Maybe that was the only time I did make her happy!" His refusal to remarry was interpreted as a sign of great love in the family, but there was also a sense of atonement surrounding his decision. I think dadi surprised dada by leaving a hollow in his heart which was never filled. In a way, her absence was more pronounced in my dad, his siblings, and dada's life than her presence had ever been.

The conversations between dada and my dad, and my uncles and aunts, were always formal queries such as, "How is Monu? Is Alam suffering from asthma? Do you remember Mr. so-and-so who was my colleague in Comilla?" My mom laughed and told my dad, "Why can't you people chat and talk normally? Your conversations are like the ones people have in offices, not in their homes!" Dada was neither too affectionate nor too stern with us. More than fear, there was a distance between us and indeed with my cousins as well, and no one knew how to overcome it. The only physical contact we had was when we touched his feet for salaam and he held his palm over our heads. I never saw him being affectionate with his children. I remember his voice and demeanor being softer and more loving toward "Tommy," the stray dog who roamed around the house and was fed regularly but never made too many demands and kept his distance as he sensed our fear of him.

If the expression of love and affection was missing from my dadabari, it was fully compensated for in my nanabari, my maternal grandparents' place, in the heart of urban Dhaka, full of exciting chatter and events that my uncles initiated. As soon as we reached their home on College Street, which would be every other day, my nani's face lit up and she said to my mom, "Buri [a term of endearment], you are here!" with amazement and joy, even though she saw us every other day. The house, the people, the surroundings, all belonged to a different world because both my nana and nani were as urban and cosmopolitan as it was possible to be in their time. Born and reared in Dhaka, with no ties to their ancestral villages, their relatives still lived in old Dhaka, in the narrow alleys of Bangsal, Shatrowza, and Kaltabazar, where the mazelike houses accommodated huge families, and the twists and turns of the stairs never ceased to surprise me. My nana, an English literature graduate, worked for the Pakistan High Commission, a job that took him to Kolkata, Rangoon, and other exotic locations. At one time he used to play the violin. I only saw pictures of him playing the violin, looking youthful and handsome, so different from the bearded man with the dark mark on his forehead from regular prayers and the ill-fitting long shirts that I witnessed. He had made his wife ride in an uncovered horse carriage and taken her to Darjeeling for their honeymoon, causing a ruckus in the family as it was an ultramodern act for the time. I remember him driving a black Volkswagen Beetle and taking us to visit relatives during Eid. The Volkswagen episodes were not too classy as all of us—nani, uncles, my mom, and I—had to fit in the little egg-shaped car, and I even remember transporting a goat for qurbani once. I mostly remember my nana with his beard and a cap on his head coming back from the mosque, often with sweets—usually jilapi—for us, intensely watching movies on TV, both Bangla and English, or music programs, especially classical ones, and blowing his hukka, as the noise of the bubbling water took over and the air filled with the smell of strong nicotine, compelling us to steal a puff when he left his seat. I have heard stories about how he sang well enough to perform in small gatherings, but I only knew him after he became religious following retirement. I remember him diligently leaving for the mosque five times a day, and my nani and mom getting upset when he would go for tabligh, roaming door to door in the countryside to teach people about proper

Islam. Nani used to cry, "I am afraid to sleep by myself, I am afraid of the dark, I hate putting on the mosquito net," while nana would retort, "It is gunah [sin] to say such things," and pacify her by making me stay with her at night. From the violin-playing, cricket-loving movie buff, he became someone opting to wear his pajama ankle-high and share food with everyone from the same plate during tabligh.

My nani was beautiful and stylish, and often compared to Madhubala, the legendary actress. She was married off when she was only fifteen. My nana attempted to prepare her for the SSC, the board exam after the tenth grade, but she was not interested in continuing her boring education, and in any case the impending pregnancy put a stop to all such efforts. I still remember her practicing her signature in English, and especially going over the "J" for Jaheda, when she had to take money out of her bank account, her eyebrows puckered in concentration. Regardless of her lack of schooling, she was able to hold her own in any conversation about any topic. The religious transformation of my nana included tagging nani along, who I suspect followed the rituals of regular prayers and fasting more out of obligation than love. I remember my nani getting ready to go out for a visit or to a wedding, inserting a blob of artificial hair in her bun to make it bigger, putting on her string of pearls that she obtained from Mecca during the hajj, choosing and wearing her saree with great care, and then reluctantly donning her burqa and tying a scarf while making sure her hair didn't get messed up. Her burqa was never the ready-made black one, but tailor-made in a sophisticated color like light blue, with attractive buttons and matching scarf that did not fully cover her black hair, which she never needed to dye. She was scared of ghosts, snakes, and the afterlife. She used to murmur during wuzu, "Please Allah, stick my feet to the poolserat [the threadlike bridge everyone will have to cross on the Day of Judgment]!" I remember laughing at it without comprehending the real fear behind this plea.

I started life with my nana and nani as my mother had gone to Sussex for her master's, leaving six-month-old me with my grandparents for a year and a half. My father remained in Dhaka and continued teaching at Dhaka University, except for a brief visit to my mother. As a single man he was perceived as being incapable of taking care of a child, so I lived with my grandparents. He visited me every day and woke me up from sleep, much to the annoyance of my ayah and nani. Nani always laid a greater claim on me than my sister or cousins, saying, "I brought you up!" All my memories of them come from much later in the College Street house where they moved after retirement and lived until they died just when I crossed my teenage years. Unlike my dada's place, nana's place was full of people when I was a kid—my uncles, their friends, various relatives, tenants and neighbors who dropped by—but gradually my uncles left for America for higher studies or jobs, robbing the place of much of its excitement and buzz.

The two-story house on College Street was smack in the urban heart of Dhaka, almost every inch of land used for the house, leaving only a narrow strip for a garden with a guava tree and a few other bushes and small trees. The house had three bedrooms, all of them unusually spacious, a huge living and dining area, and a wide balcony circling all the rooms. I loved the balcony, which was big enough to let us play badminton when we were small. The front of the house led to a view of a concrete jungle, the neighbors' house so close we could actually chat with them without raising our voices. The back of the house opened onto a wide field, with the teachers' training college at its edge. The unbounded rear of the house was always swept with a pleasant breeze, even on hot summer days, especially the balcony at the back. One side of the balcony was covered with pink bougainvillea, and afternoon tea was often served in its privacy. My nana and uncles liked to pray on the cool balcony rather than in the stuffy rooms in the summer months. I played many games on that balcony and many of our family pictures were taken in the bright airy space. It was on that very balcony, during the Liberation War, that I slipped out with my doll and had a conversation with a Pakistan Army officer who was staying at the teachers' training college and cleaning his gun. I have heard over and over how my mother started looking for me, heard my voice from the balcony, and came and snatched me inside. We had moved to my grandparents' house, leaving our comparatively unsafe university quarters, the target of the Pakistan Army's wrath, during the Liberation War. I remember my uncles cutting and pasting paper strips on windows to prevent glass from shattering during the bombings, and myself rushing downstairs during the sirens, my mother stuffing cloth in my mouth to make sure I wouldn't bite my tongue if I was terrified of the noise. Too young to be afraid, I only remember the eerie silence and my mother's palm closing over my mouth.

Unlike my uncles from my father's side—who lived in cities other than Dhaka, which meant that I only enjoyed spurious contact with my cousins—my interactions with my mother's younger brothers were more intense and regular until all of them, one by one, left for America. I have plenty of memories of their wit and sarcasm, especially when they came up with funny and appropriate names for hapless friends and relatives. "Here comes Rhino!" they said and I struggled to check my laughter as the unsuspecting cousin, who crossed the street without looking to his sides and charged ahead, showed up. When I was four years old I made the terrible mistake of calling a friend of my uncle's, a tall lanky man who moved his head too often, tiktiki (lizard) uncle, as I failed to grasp that it was not his real name.

By the time I was seven, two of my uncles had left for the U.S., the remaining one was always playing cricket, nanabari had become dull and lifeless, and my grandparents eagerly awaited our visit to brighten their day. There was no one and nothing to play with at nanabari for me or my sister as my mother chattered on, my father usually absent from such visits. There was a box made of walnut wood, light brown with an intricate design that opened when I pulled a strip to its side, a mechanism not apparent to the naked eye. The box, which was meant for precious jewelry, stood lazily over a bunch of old magazines on the center table. There was a silver paandan, made for betel leaves and associated ingredients, that I was allowed to play with. The shiny hexagon opened and revealed a tray, underneath which there were six cute boxes that could be detached and taken out of the box, revealing a second layer to store betel leaves. I remember those two boxes occupying a great deal of my time and attention. All the other beautiful objects I wanted to lay my hands on were locked securely in a glass case and all the affection my nani had for me was not enough to melt her heart to allow me to touch any of her precious possessions. A number of papier-mâché knick-knacks from Burma, shaped like owls and ducks, were deemed insignificant enough to be left out in the open. There was also a huge colorful lamp, made of camel skin, that glowed and became translucent when lit. There was a grandfather clock that needed to be wound up every week and which chimed every hour on the hour. Just before the Friday prayers, either my nana or youngest uncle, chhotu, would stand quite unsafely on a rickety table balanced against the windowsill, take out the key which opened the glass cover of the clock, and start winding. A number of plates, glasses, and cups were similarly revered, only to be taken out when special guests came. There was the famous red carpet—specially ordered and made by prisoners in the Dhaka jail, with geometric designs lacking a center, quite postmodern for a carpet—which was rolled out only during Eid or when my uncles came home from America. The sound of the cupboards opening and closing, the delicate tinkle of glass objects, and the rolling and unrolling of the carpet were signals of an impending event and the only exciting time to visit nanabari.

One of the huge events in my life was when my mother's elder brother, whom I called boro mamu, or eldest uncle, returned from Karachi, where he was trapped during the Liberation War. I had only heard stories and seen pictures of Raj and Munmun, my cousins, a couple of years older than me. They had all ended up in a refugee camp at the end of the war and arrived in Dhaka unharmed after spending a couple of very inconvenient months, nani crying and praying every day until they arrived safely. My first memory of them is the excited shriek from my mom as my third uncle, Reza, gave her the good news. We were at the TSC (Teacher-Student Center at Dhaka University), listening to a concert by one of the first modern Bengali bands, The Ugly

Phases, for whom Reza played the tambourine, dressed in his cuffed shirt and tight pants. I was eager to meet Raj and Munmun, my long-awaited cousins, but my elation did not last long, a little dampened by jealousy as they got so much attention after having been trapped in enemy territory for the full nine months of the war and then some, and also because they had settled in Chittagong where my uncle worked for Lever Brothers. He often visited Dhaka for official meetings, bringing us cartons of soap from Lever Brothers, the yellow and green bars only to be used for washing clothes. I never got to spend much time with my cousins as they only visited Dhaka once or twice a year, and by the time they moved to Dhaka, it was time for me to leave the city.

My uncle had selected his bride by overruling his mother's non-approval and my nani and aunt had kept the common Bengali tradition of ill-will between mother-in-law and daughter-in-law alive even though they had only lived together temporarily, that too for less than a year. What had seemed like an outright rebellion on Aziz uncle's part became very common by the time my three younger uncles got married, each with whomever they wanted to, nana, nani, and my mom happy enough and a little relieved at not having to go through the hassle of finding a bride—the unending delicate dance balancing social status and family prestige with the search for an impressive young woman who would make everyone happy.

My mom's second brother, Shafiq—the one immediately her younger who was closest to her, the one I call Shammu bhayya—inherited my nana's musical genes. He sang classical songs on Radio Pakistan, then on Radio Bangladesh, and finally Bangladesh Television. The programs for classical music came on very late at night, and I remember being poked and prodded to open my eyes to see my uncle on television. My dad tried to scare me by saying, "Shammu will be stuck inside the television forever! How can he ever get out?" Probably six or seven years old at the time, I had outgrown such lame jokes. Shammu was the star student of the family, studying at BUET (Bangladesh University of Engineering and Technology), and he soon left for Abu Dhabi, and a year later for the U.S. He maintained his love for music by carrying on his musical stints with his troupe, including his wife Ayesha who is from Bombay. While Shammu bhayya teased me a lot, my third uncle Reza treated me very specially, even as he worried everyone to death with his rowdy band and pot-smoking friends and late-night parties. I remember him rushing to my mom, yelling "Apa! Save me!" before his exams, to get help in history, Bengali, and whatever subject she could assist with, and he really did need help as my mother always expressed surprise when he passed instead of failing as she thought he deserved. No one had high or really any hopes for him, but he stunned everyone by leaving for America during his undergraduate years. The story of his American quest sounds like a fairytale at this time, when America has a much harsher attitude toward immigration.

One night, playing with his band at the Hotel Intercontinental (which became the Sheraton and then the Ruposhi Bangla), he was accosted by an American gentleman, Mr. Turner, who was moved by his performance. Nostalgic for Western music, he had become a regular guest at their concerts, and grandly offered to fulfill any wish my uncle made. My uncle promptly wanted a sponsorship to go to America and, to his surprise, Mr. Turner agreed. I remember the flustered reaction of my parents and grandparents, the shocked disbelief in the eyes of my scholarly Shammu bhayya when he said, "How can he leave for America before me?" and the adoration and worship of my youngest uncle as this act validated Reza's rebel lifestyle. My dad predicted, "It's a gamble! Either he will be cured or become a complete hippie!" Uncle did have a couple of hippie friends, and one of their mothers would come and cry to my nani quite regularly for a decade or so. It was the desperate pleadings of my uncle—I remember him holding my mom's legs until he extracted a promise of money— that finally melted the heart of my nana, nani, boro mamu, and mom, who all drew on their savings to pay for his fare. Of course, his fairytale was shattered by Mr. Turner's harsh expectations that he should keep his hours, act responsibly, and maintain his room properly. The kindly Mrs. Turner was far too nice to the Bengali young man who had left the comfort of his home for the first time ever, and in the end Reza uncle did not do too badly for himself. In the early seventies, it was that easy to migrate to America! America graciously offered Reza uncle the opportunity to learn, to struggle, to have adventures, and to be part of the American fabric so vehemently that his identity is wrapped up more in New York than in Dhaka. We laughed at his distress on his recent transfer to Vancouver from New York, as he could not imagine living anywhere but New York, a city to which he came when he was twenty and never left. America succeeded in bringing him into the system, making an accountant out of a musician, making a husband and father out of a true bohemian, but the irresponsible and funny and laid-back uncle I knew keeps peeking out once in a while in his misjudgments about the practical aspects of life, inappropriate remarks and lame jokes at social gatherings, and lack of a sense of direction and history of getting lost on every road trip.

My youngest uncle, Sunny—whom we call "chhotu," which means little—became a star in his own right. He was following the footsteps of Reza in his choice of friends, partying, and lack of interest in studies. Instead of music, his passion in life was cricket. Nobody took his sporting life seriously, ready to chide him when it interfered with his studies. He played everywhere, on the grounds nearby and at the university with his friends, venturing to larger and larger fields. As a student in the zoology department, he played for Dhaka University, and also played for one of the clubs, the Azad Boys Club, so that reports of his matches—sometimes his catches (he was the wicket keeper) and his injuries—ended up in the newspapers. Everything changed when he was selected to play for the national team. My nana was proud of him and the only one who eagerly went to watch his matches at the stadium. We basked in the glory of being recognized as his nieces in the neighborhood, at the university, and among our friends, but neither I nor my sister was interested in watching his matches, keeping up only with the scores. My mom watched cricket on television, but going to the stadium to watch cricket was part of her premarital life, my dad being uninterested in any games or sports. Chhotu's star status, however, did not free him from the burden of earning a living. He worked long hours in a bank, trying to squeeze out whatever time he could for practice. He couldn't get enough time off for his matches, often lying about his health as an excuse to miss office and play a match. He dreaded playing well and being praised in the newspapers as he was caught red-handed quite a few times by being the man of the match.

Eventually he migrated to America, leaving his passion behind. The more recent recognition of cricket players as professional sportsmen, and the test status of the Bangladesh team and the country's elation at their unexpected wins (and deflation at their cringe-worthy losses), are a sad reminder of how a position on the national team offered no financial security only a few decades ago and a player at that level had to leave the country in search of a better life.

All my uncles still fondly recount how they used to get hit by nana, nana breaking an umbrella on them (and sparing his only daughter), but my own memories of being disciplined are filled with confusion and pain. I remember being locked in the bathroom for accidentally breaking something, and promising not to cry, begging to be let out. Everything in the house was considered precious and breaking anything was tantamount to sin. "Why did you touch the vase? Look how you have chipped the corners. You cannot play in the afternoon. Go to the bathroom and keep quiet until I let you out!" my mother screamed with anger as I retreated to the bathroom, praying under my breath that I wouldn't encounter any cockroaches during my punishment. More than the humiliation, what baffled me about being beaten by my mother was the logic behind the proportionality of punishment as it didn't reflect the gravity of what I had done but rather the anger I had aroused in her. After we temporarily moved to nanabari while my father was doing his PhD in Delhi for four years when I was in grade seven to ten, the beatings ceased as my grandparents or my uncle intervened, saying, "Leave the children alone, you are far too strict," during the disciplinary sessions. My mom is such a persuasive teacher so I always wondered why she needed to beat us to get through to us. If anything, the beatings made me realize how vulnerable grown-ups can be, as the moment I stopped being afraid of getting hit I stopped being afraid of my mom altogether.

I resented even more the teasing of my uncles when it came at the expense of my dad's solid rural background, which my uncles found alien and amusing compared to their own exposure to urban and foreign environments. "How can you survive in a mud house without electricity and television?" they badgered, as tears welled up in my eyes. As my uncles and my mom had spent considerable time outside Bangladesh and were educated in Kolkata and Rangoon, in addition to having an Urdu-speaking background, they were not prototypical Bengalis. What my mother prided on as cultural superiority felt like not fitting in with everyone else to me and often became disturbing as my friends relayed the comments they heard from their mothers about my mother's eccentric sense of fashion. "Your mother wears large earrings! Why is her anchal so short? Why does she buy so many sarees?" were constant interrogations I heard on the playground. I remember my hesitation to switch to Urdu if I ran into my uncles or cousins in public places, muttering an awkward, "Bhalo?" and avoiding conversation, because in the seventies Urdu was the language of the enemy and I did not want to portray myself as fraternizing with enemy culture. If I had only known that I just needed to wait thirty more years when Hindi television, such as Zee TV, would take over Bangladesh and everyone would be speaking in a strange combination of Hindi and English, Hinglish, and would no longer bother to give us a second glance! I have realized with shock that my Bangla peppered with English words seamlessly fits into the Bangla spoken in Dhaka now. Chatting or texting with Zara, my friend's daughter, has made me aware of not only how little I have in common with the culture she is growing up in, but also how much more familiar the other parts of the world are to her compared to me. However, I do miss the elegance of the rounded sounds and cringe at the clashes with the angular Hindi tones and the square English words jutting out of the smooth landscape of my language.

Home

"I can see my friends outside! Can I go out now?" I would ask and my mom would respond by shoving a bowl of porridge or some equally unpalatable snack at me and then making me change into a suitable frock for outside, subtracting precious moments from my friends and the playground at my safe abode in the university quarters. My dad, a professor at Dhaka University, and my mom, who taught at a government college, started their conjugal life at the Issa Khan Road quarters, where Dhaka University professors lived in apartments owned by the university. It was a five to ten minute walking distance from the university, with trees and open fields beckoning us to play. The dorms or halls where students lived were at a stone's throw and so was the British Council. Every playground, every tree, every pavement, every street in the university area seemed to belong to me as I wandered around safely, my parents not too concerned as long as I was with friends.

We lived in a downstairs apartment and often gardened with vigor, only to give up and abandon the project quite regularly. I remember a thorny rose bush that grew high enough to show off its deep pink small roses, safely elevated from the wandering hands of passersby and ourselves. Often there was a lot of excitement about planting seeds and putting up a fence, especially if we had helping hands who were enthusiastic, but after a few successful thefts by neighborhood kids, vendors, or servants from other households, we became indifferent toward the transgressors and lost interest in the garden. I remember watering the plants inside, on our balcony, where we grew small cactuses and various green and yellow small shrubs, which we called patabahar, my mom explaining, "Cactus doesn't need much water." She watered the smaller hanging plants with soft tiny pink and yellow flowers beyond my reach, but often lowered them for me to touch their velvety melting petals. These hanging plants were placed in makeshift pots, discarded juice containers, broken teapots, or vases that were deemed not pretty enough, all hanging from wire or secured on the half-circle of the two pillars protruding inside the balcony. The small balcony was surrounded by pale red clay pots of various shapes, leaving only a narrow strip for metal and plastic chairs. My parents often had tea there. The chairs were so low that I could not see outside if I sat down. I wanted to stand up but the chairs were semi-circular in shape and wobbled under my weight. Both the front and the longer balcony at the back were covered in wire designed in an inch-long diamond pattern. I wriggled my fingers and tried to break through the wire to touch my friend who was perched uncomfortably on a wall on the other side. The floor of the balcony, like the rest of the house, was gray and uneven, but when I squeezed my eyes narrowly, I could see patterns in it.

I slipped away from my nap in the afternoons to lie on the cold hard cement of the balcony. The sun was partially blocked because of the plants, and the patterns of light and shadow captured my imagination. I could make out a teapot, a house, a profile of a face. Quick, it changed with the sun! If I wanted to, I could hold objects in my mind and make them change shape. A few years later, I abandoned my small wooden chair and table to lie on the floor and do my homework. I no longer remember how winter felt on that balcony. Perhaps it was closed and I was not allowed to go there in the winter. I do remember the cool firm floor and the gentle breeze even on hot summer days. The balcony was a separate enclave as the door that connected the balcony to the living room was kept closed to protect the furniture from dust. I could play for hours without being afraid of eavesdroppers (my sister or maidservants) laughing at my conversations with my imaginary friend, the nice girl who adored me and whose name I no longer remember. My imaginary friend had multiple personalities which were eerily similar to my actual friends, but a lot nicer, and all of them played with me on that balcony or in the study room when my dad was not at his desk. From morning to afternoon, the balcony belonged to me, until my sister started playing in that space. I read a lot of books there, especially on long summer afternoons, oblivious to the world outside, the stillness pierced by the occasional screams of the vendors, "Sharikapor!" (cloth seller) or "Bothi dhaar!" (knife sharpener), only the moving rays forcing me to change position in the crisp solace of gray cement.

The balcony in the back was longer, but more functional, with a table in one corner where my mom ironed our clothes in the evening, and my sister's discarded high chair and pram in another corner. Both of these were soon recycled, robbing us of the furniture of the imaginary house which we stuffed with toys and where we enacted the roles of adults (we called the game "house, house," pretending to be adults and going to the office and cooking, etc.). We had little peace there because of continuous interruptions, my mom dusting things in the small cupboard, the servants asking something of my mom or going to the dining space, my dad coming in and out of his study.

Following the obligatory nap after school, I rushed out to play with my friends each afternoon. The ability to hold one's breath for a long time was a much sought-after skill, needed in kut-kut, ha-du-du, and golla chhut. Kut-kut was for girls, especially when only a few of us were around and space was limited. We could easily draw the courts anywhere, all we needed was chalk to draw on the cement so we could jump around the courts and take turns. The other two games which were girls-only were golap togor (red and white, for the flower it was named after) and rumal chor (handkerchief thief), both of them guessing games serving as warm-ups while waiting for more people to join in or played at the end of the evening when the energy was gone but no one was ready to call it a day. It was possible to cheat in golap togor, in fact it was the cheating that made the game exciting. I marvel now at the elaborate cheating mechanisms devised by five- and six-years-olds. Golla chhut and ha-du-du demanded good runners so I was not a popular person on any team. When making up the teams, the leaders did their best not to put me on theirs. I was never the one to try to get on a new tree, or to fly my swing a little higher. My aim was also terrible, and I always got the last try on shatchara, or seven stones, where one had to break the pyramid of seven stones with a tennis ball and rebuild it while the opposite team tried to stop one.

There were only two seesaws and one swing in our park so we had to take turns. To make sure everyone got their turn, we huddled together around the swing, a couple of younger kids holding the chain as if their life depended on it (and indeed it did!) and an older kid standing and using one foot to prop up the swing. Munni could push the swing sky-high with as many as five of us. I closed my eyes and held the chain so tight there were deep red marks on my palm. I looked up to Tanuja in the fluorescent green dress tirelessly paying kut-kut, lithe Munni running, Titash expertly climbing a tree, Jhuma aiming at the pile of stones to topple them in shatchara. We were generally unsupervised on the playground, though there were a few older siblings or adults walking with their children who encroached on our space and litigated our disputes, because everyone, even passersby, had the right to intervene in fights, to yell if we were doing something dangerous, or to tell us not to run around when cars were passing by.

Sometimes there was sand piled in front of our apartment building. When construction materials were scattered in the space between the two buildings or on the grass, we were not allowed to touch it, but could anyone prevent children, from toddlers to teens, from playing with the sand? We pretended that the sand was a beach. The metal water tanks at the top of each building were replaced with more permanent large cement ones. For weeks, the two abandoned metal tanks lay on the ground, the perfect place to hide or play. They became aircraft, spacecraft, hospitals, houses, or schoolrooms in turn. Scratching myself as I entered through the small opening, I remember the damp smell, the feeling of power and fear when I went to a corner and the tank swayed, and the claustrophobia when only a few of us were inside. It was fun to poke my head in and scream and listen to the echo.

My friends and I made up a game trying to guess the word from the faint echo that could be heard outside.

There were small patches of land in front of each building and between the structures, which were often turned into gardens and prohibited to children. When they were not changed into gardens, we played to our heart's content. Two bamboo poles were sprung for the badminton net and the shuttlecock was swung back and forth endlessly through the short winter afternoons. Whoever paid for the net and set it up had first dibs, but everyone took turns. If you didn't have your own racket, the person who was tightly clutching their racket and waiting impatiently had to let you borrow the cherished racket. In a resource-scarce environment, the culture of sharing went beyond family, and even family had an extended definition that included friends and neighbors. We used the terms brothers and sisters when talking about cousins; instead of the generic "cousin," we classify matrilineal and patrilineal ones, derived from aunts or uncles, but unless asked to elaborate we refer to them as brothers and sisters.

When I wasn't allowed to go outside, because it was either too early or too late, my companions were my storybooks. I got books only on special occasions—birthday, Eid, as a reward for good results, or as a sudden windfall from a relative. When I was in nursery school (pre-K), I had a tutor, Bijoy, whom I called drawing sir, who taught me handwriting and drawing. Neither my penmanship nor my drawing improved, but I remember my tutor's joy when I stood first in nursery and the huge pile of books he brought me as a gift. It was such a treasure! I could hardly carry the whole bunch by myself. It took me weeks to finish the books, and I had a shelf assigned in the rickety bamboo bookcase that held magazines and less important books and did not let anyone (my mom or my dad) put anything other than my books in that bookcase. My books soon took over the entire bookcase, as I jealously looked up to the wooden ones with glass doors where the adult books were housed. Unless we were fighting and not on speaking terms, it was not the norm to deny anyone anything, a book to read or a toy to play with, as we were taught to share everything with everyone.

Despite my agony and tears over torn covers and loose pages and colored marks in my books after they made the rounds to friends and were returned to me, I could not not share books with my friends. I'm sure I caused similar pain to others. I loved the Russian books that were readily and cheaply available with wonderful illustrations, books such as *Clever Masha, The Rainbow Flower, Russian Fairy Tales, Rain and Stars, Kashtanka, The Malachite Casket, and of course, The Story of the Pencil and the One Who Could Do It All*. I remember my first heartbreak over "the amphibian man," who had to choose between living on land or water and had to give up his love. While Russian books were cheap and plentiful, Indian books were expensive and rare. How we longed for Detective Feluda who seemed like an approachable older cousin and the unobtrusive genius Professor Shonku, both of them characters by Satyajit Ray who still feel real to me! My mom once brought ten Satyajit Ray books for me from a single trip to Kolkata, perhaps the most cherished gifts I ever got. I still have a couple of books from that stack that I have carried across the continents for over twenty years.

I vividly remember reading Leela Mojumdar for the first time. She was the writer who made me aware of the beauty of language, how certain words made one squirm in delight, how one could read the same story again and again for sheer pleasure. My friend Titash left frantic messages for me during one of my dadabari trips. When I went to see her, she told me that she had discovered a gold mine. She had come across this wonderful book and had to return it within a day or two and she wanted me to read it. The writer was Leela Mojumdar, someone I'd never read before. From the moment I read "Podipishir Bormi Baksho" (the Burmese box that belonged to aunt) I was hooked on her stories. A few years later, "Buro Angla" by Abanindranath Thakur, where a thumb-sized character has the adventure of a lifetime flying on a swan, made me rethink nature as I fell in love with every animal and bird in the story. Getting hold of Indian books was not easy in my early childhood, and even Bengali classical literature by Indian writers such as Upendrakishore Ray was rarely available in mainstream bookstores. Thankfully, from the early eighties on, the market was flooded with Indian books, although they cost three times more than local books.

I had to wait until my teens for Bangladeshi writers to seriously focus on literature for young adults which was not educational fables. The wait was long, but the reward worth it. I remember well the suspense of "Operation Kakonpur," the wonder of "Nuliachhorir Shonar Pahar" and "Hariye Jabar Thikana," and the breathless excitement of reading "Dipu Number Two" in *Kishore Bangla*, the first-ever monthly paper for youth. Shahriar Kabir and Zafar Iqbal understood children, especially adolescents, with a spirit and vigor we hadn't known before. While Shahriar Kabir brought adventure and politics into our world, Zafar Iqbal ignited our imagination with science fiction celebrating the humanity in mankind, robots, and aliens alike.

Titash, who introduced me to many wonderful writers (she had several older siblings), Jhuma, who lived upstairs, Mohua, in the building in front, Papia, whom I saw in class every day, Munni, who could hold her breath for the longest time ever, and Amatul, who had perfect aim for the seven stones game, were all around whenever I felt like playing. There were boys as well—Bulu, Ratan, Limon, Shaker, Usama, and Amin—with whom we played and fought over space just as their football field encroached on our space. The boys played ha-du-du, shatchara, or tilo-express with us, occasionally inviting us to their football games. Football and cricket were male games when I was growing up. Often the older boys started a match and boys of our age were reduced to playing with us for lack of space.

If there were too many people, tilo-express was the obvious choice because it could accommodate many people without needing much room. It was like hide-and-seek, with the excitement enhanced by the rules that the seeker had to call out the person by name (Jhuma express, or Papia express!) and if the hider touched the seeker (tilo!), the seeker lost the round. To confuse the seeker, we exchanged clothes with each other, a scarf, a bangle, sometimes the entire outfit. Amin hid in a tree once and when the seeker stood on a bench at the foot of the tree to get a better look at the field, two skinny legs came down and touched his shoulder, a muffled tilo uttered amid our breathless excitement. There were no limits to finding a good hiding place—inside bushes, in a dry drain, the narrow space between the L-shaped row of garages and the boundary wall of our school, Udayan Bidyalaya, where people dumped garbage¬¬—anywhere would do.

Amatul and Amin taught us how to climb the roofs of garages. It was difficult, one had to climb an adjacent tree, and if one were lucky enough to find the corner garage empty and unlocked, one had to hold on to the door for extra support. Compared to the krishnachura tree right across the garages, which had wide welcoming branches making room for at least four kids, the slender trees beside the garages were a challenge. But if I could make it to the top, I could stare down at the cowardly kids, defying and laughing at the face of the guard who kept telling us to get down. I spent a number of afternoons on the krishnachura, gathering courage to make the leap, looking greedily at the excitement on the garage roof. Soon we discovered that the easiest way to go up and come down was through the back of the garage, where garbage lay stacked up, since we only had to stand on the soft high pile, put one leg on the Udayan wall, and there we were! To get down we only had to jump on to the mound of garbage, being careful to dust off the incriminating evidence.

I had a cardboard box full of toys, much to the envy of my friends. Mostly it was filled with discarded odds and ends, rather than manufactured toys. I remember a red purse, a clutch with a silver design missing on one side, which was an essential accessory when I pretended to be a grown-up. There were a lot of handmade cloth dolls, whose names kept changing according to my mood, and a huge supply of sarees for them, made from rejected clothes. When my mom took me to the tailor's shop, the highlight was collecting the colorful materials falling off the huge scissors, ideal to deck out my dolls. There were plenty of clay pots and pans to play "ghor ghor" (house, house). A small aluminum pot was equivalent to a treasure. There was a lot of wooden stuff along with cheap plastic materials. I don't remember playing with cars, although my mom tells me the story of a red car I fancied, one that belonged to my cousin, which I found more appealing than my own blue one. The unattractive local plastic dolls couldn't hold a torch to the small cloth ones, with which we held extravagant productions of marriage ceremonies. Often all you needed was an older sister, cousin, or a helping hand at home, willing to make a doll with rags, twigs, and thread. We designed elaborate family trees for our dolls that changed in tune with their circumstances. Somebody once made a doll for me which had a button sown on the back of the head to represent a bun. Usually thread—or if one was lucky, wool—was used to make the hair. The most majestic of my dolls were two large jute dolls—one for me and one for my sister, bought from Karika, the upscale shop at the time—which could be bent and held many different ways, never losing their thin red thread smile as they sat contentedly on the windowsill. I got my first Barbie doll when I was almost twelve, past the age of playing with dolls, when my uncles living abroad had got married and my aunts had the sense to get us the right kinds of gifts. I enviously looked at my five years younger sister playing with her Barbie, being too old to play but refusing to give up my doll and my share of accessories.

There were two tin banks for me and my sister, oval-shaped, bright blue with a colorful design, and a key to unlock the bottom and take out the coins. We were fascinated with the keys, sometimes misplacing them and making the banks useless. I remember shaking the banks over and over to get the few remaining coins and failing. Because we fought over toys, my mom got us two Ludo boards, making us the pampered kids in the neighborhood with such duplication. The stroke of luck ended when one day, returning from work, my mom found us playing without having had lunch and tore up the board on which we were playing as a punishment. The local store outside our gate, which carried bananas, eggs, snacks, and soft drinks, enticed us with new designs of pens, pencils, and erasers along with toffee, achar (pickle), and the cheap snacks that we were not allowed to have most of the time. I remember crying for a pen with a cap shaped like a badminton racket.

The most precious toys resided on the top shelves of the showcase in the living room, which were beyond my reach. I had to be satisfied with a few opportunities to touch the two dolls that were mine every now and then. One was from Holland, all dressed up and wearing wooden shoes, who stood in her plastic covering all her life as I gazed hungrily at her. She had a scarf which I longed to take off to play with her hair, but was never allowed to do. She wore a black dress, made of velvet, and I remember how badly my palms itched for the smooth touch. Years later she disintegrated, without knowing my longing and affection, and all that remains now are her wooden shoes which my mom is still preserving. I think her name was Shirley. There was another smaller doll, a gift from my mother's Australian adviser from Sussex, which stood in a box with layers of clothes. If I could have taken her out of the box, I would have peeled off the layers of clothes and played with her for hours. But I could only look at her from a distance and imagine how it would feel to play with her. On rare occasions, my mom handed her to me and I took off all the clothes and dressed her right back. I did this about twenty times. She too disappeared without a trace and left the feeling that I never got to know her. I took my revenge playing with Shehnaz, the large curly-haired doll my mom got me from England. I played with Shehnaz so often with such vigor that her limbs were torn apart and she soon lost her foreign status and stood with the local cloth and jute dolls dressed in my newborn sister's cast-off clothes.

Nausheen's birth was the first trauma of my five-year-old life that affected me deeply. I experienced a range of emotions—love, hate, jealousy, ownership, pride—jumbled up and pulling at me from different directions with the arrival of the toylike chubby new baby. I had no clues of this major event about to take place, only a premonition of something weird, when I discovered a soft toy, a blue-and-white striped stuffed animal unlike any real animal, hidden amid clothes. I assumed it was for me, only to be ticked off by my mom, "This is not for you!" I remember holding it in amazement and wondering who it could be for. My dad asked me the night of my sister's birth, "Do you want a sister or a brother?" I chose a sister and I got one. She was looking everywhere with her round eyes, the first day at the clinic, a healthy eight-pound baby who was favorably compared to my measly six-and-a-half-pound skeletal self when I was born. What I remember from the visits to the clinic was the swing where I rushed after an obligatory glance at the baby and my mom surrounded with relatives, all of them so happy. During my mom's labor, I stayed with her cousins, Nishat and Sylvi, who helped me cut out paper dolls and their dresses, and played with me and kept me distracted. The swing, the squishy baby, the round eyes that held more curiosity than tears were all good omens—but disaster could not be averted for long.

As soon as my sister was brought home—meaning College Street where we stayed for forty days according to the custom requiring a mother to stay at her parents' home after childbirth—I got chicken pox. I was deemed too dangerous to be near the baby or even my mother. I was smuggled into a separate room in a lonely cot (I'm sure I wasn't allowed to sleep by myself, but that's how I remember it) covered by a mosquito net, a makeshift quarantine to protect the new baby from my germs. The tidal influx of visiting relatives was given the choice to see either me or the new baby. Of course, the new baby won hands down. I remember hearing voices, feeling left out and hungry for human company. I missed my mom, but I missed food even more. At the time, the common practice was to deny a weak and ill person all protein—no meat, no fish, no eggs. I'm not sure if it was doctor's orders or if the caution was based on local custom. Never in my five-year old life had I eaten such bad food—insipid, colorless, tasteless—without coaxing from my mom. My mom only came and looked at me from outside the mosquito net. My nani fed me, urging all the time, "Finish the food quickly, I have to bathe the new baby." My uncle, who was studying at BUET, came to lunch late, and often took pity and fed me a bite or two from his food when everyone else was sleeping. Nani caught us once and charged him with trying to kill me. The other memory I have is of crying for "dry cake," a sort of cookie, and being overjoyed at the prospect of eating something tasty when my wish was granted. But as I was about to take a bite, my nani blurted out from the blue, "Doesn't this have eggs?' I remember the anticipation, the excitement, and the ultimate betrayal in detail. My mom, standing at a safe distance, tried to appeal, "Maybe a tiny bite?" but nani vigorously shook her head. Maybe my disdain for following rules had an unhappy root there.

Although my relationship with my sister started in turmoil, I was acutely aware of my enhanced prestige and status as the elder sister. I wanted her name to rhyme with mine, but I already had a doll called Shehnaz. At first I didn't like the name, Nausheen, my mother chose, because I feared being bullied for the name as the Bengali pronunciation of the Persian name sounded like having nine horns (Nausheen: noy shing). Already I had heard, "Your mom left you when you were a baby. She is not leaving your sister. See, she loves her more than you!" I don't remember who said it, but I remember my heart stopping at that remark. Nausheen won over my jealousy as soon as she started being responsive. When we went back to our home in the university quarters, I bragged about how she talked, sat, stood, and walked, with friends who had brothers and sisters of similar ages. I usually won the argument with Papia, my dearest friend in the building facing us, as her brother Porag was born a couple of months later than Nausheen, and was always catching up to her in talking, walking, and so on. Once, in frustration, Papia screamed at me, "I have both a brother and a sister, you only have one sister!" stunning me to the point that I couldn't even cry.

My clearest memory about the winter mornings on College Street is getting ready in my white shirt and blue skirt, while the pretty and petite Laily, Nausheen's ayah, squatted in a corner, first giving the baby an oil massage, making her purr like a cat, and then spoiling the whole effect by dressing her in a very small tight red sweater. I can still see the sweater with its blue embroidery, and the tiny opening for a neck, just a slit in the shoulders. My sister wailed endlessly and turned red, but no one showed any mercy. It was an elaborate process maneuvering the small arms of the baby, and with each movement I feared that her arms would tear off. No one shared my fears but my heart warmed toward the helpless creature who had to go through this painful ritual until the sweater became altogether too small. I have unhappy memories of being made to wear uncomfortable clothes only because they looked good. I hated rompers as you had to take them off to pee. I remember being subjected to wearing uncomfortable shoes—a pair of black closed sandals stands out in memory—which went very well with a Burmese lungi and top that my mother made me wear when I was around seven. With tears in my eyes for fear of being teased for wearing a lungi (only men wore lungi in Bangladesh), I was propped up and taken to the studio for a picture as I looked cute in the outfit. My eyes stung from the pain in my feet and every step in those beautiful black sandals was torture, but my mom insisted, "How can the sandals hurt when they fit you? Now *smile!*" I looked at the pleading photographer and my irritated mom, and promised to take revenge by not smiling. We still have that picture, me all dressed up, looking out with sad teary eyes, the sandals peeking out from under the lungi dress. While for me it is evidence of insensitive parenting, my mom interprets it as my obstinacy, a sign that was clear even at that age.

My mom's frequent visits to her parents' house on College Street became a problem for me as she was always tagging me and my sister along. I resented giving up my precious afternoon playtime with friends, when my mom often hauled me off the playground, put me in a nice (often uncomfortable) dress, and took me to my grandparents' place or some other relative's or friend's home that my parents regularly visited. How I hated those visits! To be dressed up, sitting and answering the same boring questions by grown-ups, while my friends were playing to their heart's content! The only consolation was when we went somewhere and I met someone from my own age group—and I did have cousins of the same age such as Tanya, Zafreen, and Mala—but we could not keep visiting such places day after day. The time I most resented going to relatives was Eid day, when my friends were in their new Eid dresses in large groups visiting door to door in each building and tasting the aromatic shemai, jorda, and chotpoti, part of the Eid feast. If we were not in Kuliarchar, we would definitely have to go to College Street, leaving the fun and frolicking behind.

We went out a lot to visit people such as my grandparents, other relatives, and friends of my parents, constituting the bulk of our social life, with only rare ventures to Chinese restaurants, a few visits outside the city, and no movies, no amusement parks, nothing geared toward children. Rather than the social calls, the more enjoyable part was spontaneously stopping at street corners to buy snacks or fruits for our hosts or for ourselves. My mom enjoyed the cheap unhealthy snacks sold on street corners with as much relish as I did. Jhalmuri, chotpoti, and haleem never tasted as good when our mothers cooked them with so much care at home. Chotpoti is a combination of beans cooked in spices, to which are added onions, tomatoes, cilantro, and chilies, and the indispensable tamarind juice. A more expensive version had pieces of boiled eggs in it. It was incomplete without fuchka, the small airy balls made of wheat and crumbled on top. I liked to put chotpoti inside the fuchka, and adding extra tamarind juice, I put the whole fuchka inside my mouth. Haleem is a combination of various beans and meat, too fulsome and expensive for a regular snack, but it is a popular iftar food. Kabab-paratha was also a step up in the snack food chain; we could only consume it for special celebrations. All these street foods have gained elevated status as they are now served in fast-food restaurants which claim to have more hygienic practices, but nothing can match the burst of joy that was elicited by local vendors with their greasy tattered vans, ridiculously small tin plates, and water so cloudy we hesitated to wash our plates and hands in it.

The highlight when visiting relatives was riding in the rickshaw, the hot, dusty streets of Dhaka beckoning us with alluring displays of fruits and snacks on the pavements, clashing with the stench and litter. We waited for the summer holidays because of the mangoes and lychees that filled those days. The kalboishakhi, the sudden short storm that erupts in the early summer months, blew away the small unripe mangoes, which were gathered and eaten with salt, spices, and mustard oil. There are no words to describe the feeling of having kacha amer bhorta when it is raining outside. The deep green mango skin revealed the light green surface inside that turned yellow with the spices and mustard oil, and was sour and hot with sudden sweetness. Peara (guava), amra (I don't know whether there is an English word for it, it probably belongs to the guava family), and boroi (plum) were available from the end of winter. Guavas came in many shapes, from small ones that could be hidden in the palm to the size of a tennis ball. Some of them were pink inside, but most were white. They were cheap and available everywhere. The amra was a smaller oval-shaped fruit, often cut like a flower, with red spices adorning the white flesh inside. The plums could be orange or green; often the green ones were rather large. You put the whole plum in the mouth and spit out the pit. Although these could be brought home to be consumed, the pleasure of buying them on street corners and eating and talking at the same time was priceless.

Another magical fruit was jam, a deep purple oval-shaped fruit, light purple inside, a perfect combination of sweet and sour like the balance of its hues. The fruit sellers put a handful of them in a tin jar and tumbled them around with spices, then put the spicy mishmash with all its shades of purple in a piece of paper, which we ate without washing our hands yet never becoming sick. There was frequent rainfall for respite in the summer months. Just after a short burst of rain was over, when everything was much cleaner, brighter, and greener, the fruit sellers reappeared in the temporarily abandoned streets, and the sweet and sour tastes of the summer fruits became all the more mouth-watering. People gave in to temptation, as the rain disrupted the rhythm of life and allowed the excuse to be lazy.

As the heat intensified, the mangoes and lychees ripened. The sweet red mangoes were often bought in baskets, and the baskets, which had to be kept in cool places to make sure that the mangoes didn't turn too ripe, often ended up under the bed. The syrupy lychee had soft white moist flesh and a large pit, and was so sticky that my mom laid down old newspapers for us to sit on while we ate it and we had to take a shower right afterward. The huge, thorny, and frankly quite ugly jackfruit overpowered everything with its strong smell. There was the pineapple, a must during a fever or cold, the ever-present papaya, the sweet cantaloupe, and the jambura with its pink juicy flesh. The hard surface of the green kodbel was twice the size of a tennis ball, into which a hole was drilled, just enough to pour spices in and tumble it around quickly and hand over to the customer, along with two sticks to carve out the crunchy seeds and orange flesh. It always left me wanting more. Consumed both in the street and at home, kodbel were sold all over the city, making the summer air heavy with their aroma. The presence of so many vendors also meant the presence of large numbers of buyers; passersby had to share the street with buyers and sellers, and pause and become consumers on their way home.

The street food was at its best during Ramazan, the month of fasting. Temporary food stalls emerged all over the streets to sell special iftar food—accommodating the working poor who were not able to rush home for iftar—usurping walking space along the pavements, and even spilling over into the streets and obstructing rickshaws and cars. The smell of unhealthy deep-fried foods after a day of fasting made the fast worthwhile. These included peaju, made of lentil and onions, beguni, fried eggplant in bean paste, and chhola, beans so soft they melted in the mouth. Haleem was considered a special treat for iftar, because it contained meat for much-needed protein. Fruits were also refreshing after abstention from food and water the whole day. The feast of iftar overpowered the subdued mood of the fast. Restaurants ceremonially closed for the first few days of Ramazan, but soon reopened and did business surreptitiously by hanging a curtain over their doors, as if the curtain signaled their reverence for Ramazan.

In a life without the internet, gadgets, or attractive toys, and with very limited television (Bangladesh Television only offered programs from evening to midnight), books and playing outdoors were the primary sources of entertainment. The university quarters which housed the faculty had a built-in environment for promoting reading habits: at least one of our parents was a teacher, there was an abundant supply of children and young adults of all ages, and there was proximity to decent libraries, especially the British Council. Most of the books I read during my childhood were in exchange with other books from friends. There was always a deadline looming, which made me a superfast reader. The annoying part was if there was a fight with someone whose book I had borrowed but not finished. A lot of our games ended in tears with the combatants swearing not to play with each other (at least until the next afternoon), and one had to give back the book of the enemy after the ritual break-up. "Ari, Ari, Ari," the angry voice chirped, and there was nothing to do but to extend my pinky to touch hers and then walk away in agony, throwing back a half-read book, anger melting in tears with each step. By the time we made up, the unfinished book might be with someone else and I would have to wait my turn and be careful not to hear the ending when the fortunate ones were discussing it. The blessing of scarce resources bonded us, and, more importantly, taught us to appreciate the value of books.

Bangladesh in its post-liberation glory was exciting and energetic, buoyant and brimming with the spirit of optimistic nationalism. While children in America were being instructed to think of starving Bangladeshi children and not to waste food, we were slowly getting used to seeing child beggars and child labor and accepting this as the norm. Our middle-class world was filled with heated discussions about capitalism, socialism, and India and other countries' influence on Bangladeshi politics. Socialist ideology has historically held revered status in Bengali politics (both in East and West Bengal) and Soviet support during the Liberation War only made the spirit of communism more popular. The Soviet Union, however, unlike in many other regions, used mainly soft power to retain and deepen its influence in Bangladesh. Instead of blatant propaganda, we got access to a wide array of translated Soviet literature for children, both in Bengali and in English, far cheaper than British and American books. With the wonderful quality of printing and illustration, and the cheap rates, these books surfaced as the most enjoyable and popular children's books for middle- and upper-class Bangladeshi children. I still remember the Bangla translator Noni Bhoumik. Our minds were filled with stories of Masha, Katia, Ivan, and Timur, characters who seemed like friends but had unceasing adventures. I remember making the plan of setting up a club like the one Timur and his friends had. Masha became an epithet to be bestowed for any clever act among our friends. To this day, whenever I hear a Russian name I feel like I have been transported to my childhood.

Later as a student in Canada and as a teacher in Cleveland, Ohio, I met many Soviet fellow students who were equally enthusiastic about Indian movies. During the Cold War, the foreign movies most prominently allowed into the Soviet Union were Indian movies. I also remember watching a disproportionate number of Russian movies in the late seventies as the Saturday afternoon movie, when foreign movies would be shown on Bangladesh

Television. Most of the movies on the Second World War that I watched were Russian and I was astonished when later I learned of America's involvement in the Second World War, as we grew up knowing America and the Soviet Union as mortal enemies.

In our newly liberated country, the concept of revolution took center stage. I cannot remember a time when I didn't hear heated political arguments. At home, at school, and on the streets, everyone had their own opinions, which no one was shy about expressing. I don't remember being protected from these discussions. The only topic that was taboo was anything related to sex. We were encouraged to read the newspapers, which were thick and heavy, so that everyone saved the papers and sold them to the kagojwala, the junk collector, who in turn sold them to industries as raw material. Everyone got a share of the windfall income, my share ranging from a couple of taka to five taka (not worth translating into dollars as the purchasing power of five taka was two bottles of Coke until the late seventies).

The exercise of soft power by the two empires, when I was at a tender age, on balance enriched our lives. If our literary world was dominated by the Soviet Union, American television serials captured our vision and imagination. The earliest TV serial I watched breathlessly was *Land of the Giants*. Laura Ingalls made Sunday mornings special as everyone loved *Little House on the Prairie*. I remember getting bored with the goodness of *The Waltons*. We got to see most of the popular shows like *The Fugitive, The Man from U.N.C.L.E., Diff'rent Strokes, The Six Million Dollar Man, The Bionic Woman, Dallas, and Dynasty,* but we usually didn't see them at the time of their release. I think Bangladesh Television bought older serials at a cheaper rate.

I remember reading Enid Blyton and Nancy Drew, and classics like *Huckleberry Finn* and *Uncle Tom's Cabin,* but mostly I read Russian books until my teenage years. I realize now that many of the wonderful Russian stories were written by famous writers such as Chekhov. These books probably rank even now among the best of children's literature. It was easy to identify with the characters in the books, and their snow-covered world, and imagine them as friends. The illustrations were perfect, often drawn by children. I remember a photograph of a thirteen-year-old illustrator (I think her name was Olga) standing atop a tree branch, who had drawn the pictures for *Rain and Stars.* These books took us to a new realm that existed on the magical pages, sometimes glimpsed on the television screen. We were acutely aware of how different our worlds were and that we would have to grow up and leave to touch that world. Could that be one of the reasons why so many Bangladeshi people of my generation left home? The push-and-pull of migration and brain drain are the rational explanations, but I wonder about the psychological setup that prepared us for and beckoned us to a larger world. What if the world were as porous as it is today? Would we have grown up with dreams of adventures that could only take place in faraway lands?

Ancestral home in Kuliarchar

A. H. Sayeedullah, the writer's paternal grandfather,
with his children

Rafia Begum, the writer's grandmother

Abba & dada in Kuliarchar

Habibur Rahman & Jaheda Rahman, the writer's maternal
grandparents

Humaira Momen and Hafizur Rahman, the writer's mother and
youngest uncle

Dr. Nurul Momen and Mrs. Humaira Momen, the writer's parents

College Street balcony

Family picture with parents and sister

Family picture with extended family

Learning

Was Aleya, the daughter of the maid who worked next door, my first friend? I remember playing with her and hiding our friendship from my mom, who was not happy when I played with the maid's daughter. Our worlds diverged when I started going to school and she didn't. I remember her sad eyes when I showed off my new books, pencils, and the small black-and-white suitcase with my name painted in white. I had a blue plastic water bottle, shaped like a camera with the protruding white lens doubling as the glass. I forgot all about Aleya with the excitement of school. I don't remember my first day at school, but I do remember being tested for admission, being asked to recite A to Z. Udayan Bidyalaya, my school, was practically an extension of our para, only a common wall separating the two areas. A lot of my classmates in school were already my friends, and even a number of teachers were known faces. I ran to school, racing against the bell at eight a.m., catching up with Jhuma, Usama, and Shaker on my way. One of the advantages of living so near was that I got to stay there as long as I wanted to after school was over. We needlessly hung around with friends, waiting for their parents or cars, as if this were our responsibility. The spillover benefit was that if ever I got detention and had to stay for an extra hour, my mother could not detect it because I came home late anyway.

While I made new friends at school, my relationship with my old friends from para, especially those who ended up going to the nearby University Laboratory School, soured over fights about the superiority of our respective schools. While ULab was older, bigger, and highly subsidized, Udayan strove to make up for its crammed space and lack of adequate playgrounds by emphasizing English and a stringent battery of tests. Our fights were quite intense as Udayan and ULab, both within the university campus perimeter, were the destinations of nearly all school-going children residing on campus. I remember screaming at Ratan at the top of my voice, "Your school is nothing compared to ours!" Although the claims were far from reality, the tin roofs, the packed classrooms, the sandy patches that qualified as playgrounds, the dusty narrow paths covered with bricks, the rooms where we struggled to lay claim on the back rows, the white-and-blue uniforms and the red sweaters in winter, the punishment of standing outside if we were late for the national anthem, and the smelly toilets that did not close properly, all are etched in my heart as part of the most desirable place on earth.

Our semi-private schools were a tad more costly than the government ones; all through the seventies and eighties, only a handful of English-medium private schools, which were quite expensive, existed in Dhaka. Except for the very rich, all the government and private schools sought to produce students who would be at par with those graduating from English-medium schools. In the last couple of decades, the overwhelming number of English-medium schools has dwarfed Bangla-medium schools, attracting students despite their high tuition. The disastrous effect is that the quality of Bangla-medium schools has deteriorated because now the school system is two-tiered: the aspiring middle-class and the rich who can afford English-medium schools for their children, and those who cannot. The current generation is more comfortable and adept in English not only because of their schooling but also because of their overall exposure to television, movies, and technology, but by the same token they have given up on Bengali language, literature, and arts as the price to assimilate and participate on the world stage. Side by side, however, the celebration of Bengali culture, at least on the surface, has become more colorful and luscious, penetrating all spheres of society. The students of English-medium schools like to wear saree and bangles and eat panta bhat and organize the Boishakhi Mela, but they do not read the Bengali classics.

Our school library was a makeshift half a room divided by bookshelves, where we also had our geography elective class, as classrooms kept cramming up and becoming scarce. Only students of the eighth, ninth, and tenth grades were allowed to borrow books, while the rest had to sit and read in the minuscule library. We had music and art classes, and some years, with sudden enthusiasm, a gym class was part of the schedule. The tiny dusty playground did not have enough space for gym or recess for even a few classes together. Our breather occurred in religion class, which no one took seriously, or music and art classes. We were mean to religion teachers who lacked the sophisticated education of other teachers. There was one teacher who insisted on separate seating for girls and boys; just before his class we paired up with boys, forcing him to spend half the class time straightening our seating arrangement. The annual sports had to be held on the university playground while the annual milad (commemorating the birthday of the Prophet) and cultural programs took place at the TSC (Teacher-Student Center) belonging to Dhaka University.

The lack of extracurricular activities was made up for by the cultural rituals taking place all around us on the university campus. We had a yearly sojourn to Shaheed Minar on 21st February to commemorate our Language Martyrs' Day. February is the most revered month in the Bengali calendar, at least in Bangladesh. In 1952, when the newly formed East Pakistan rebelled against the imposition of the single national language of Urdu, the government tried to suppress the spontaneous Language Movement by spraying bullets at the students' processions. The martyrs—Salam, Barkat, Rafiq, Jabbar, and numerous unknown ones—laid the foundations upon which Bangladeshi identity blossomed and thrived. The twenty-four-year-old failed political experiment called Pakistan, geographically divided between the eastern and western parts with India in the middle, imploded in 1971 with the Liberation War. The demand that Bengali, the language of the majority in the east, should have the status of a national language was conceded at last in 1956, but by that time the differences in cultural identity between the two parts of Pakistan had become clearer, sharper, and more conflictual, and the unstable political system—peppered with military dictatorship, sometimes closeted, sometimes out in the open—attempted not to negotiate but to crush the legitimate political demands of East Bengal over and over.

Every 21st February, we formed long lines at dawn in the late winter morning. We took part in Probhat Ferry, the morning procession leading to nearby Shaheed Minar. The tradition was to wear white with sprinkles of red and black. We started out wearing our school uniforms, without our shoes, holding bouquets of flowers (made by each student from flowers gathered from neighborhood trees), and solemnly walked for twenty minutes from our school to Shaheed Minar, the spot where the martyrs had been killed and the sculpture sanctifying the space had been erected. Students at the Art Institute painted complex decorations, alpona, on the streets, and quotes from poems, songs, and essays were painted on the walls opposite and leading to Shaheed Minar. We formed a line and walked past the residential halls of Dhaka University (Jagannath Hall and Salimullah Muslim Hall), passing BUET (Bangladesh University of Engineering and Technology) on the right, until we reached the revered spot. We laid down our flowers after climbing the wide stairs that led to the five structures symbolizing a mother and her four sons. It was a national holiday, and often in our school and always in our neighborhood para there would be a celebratory program, where even if I only got to sing in chorus, or occasionally recite a poem, my day was quite full.

The month of February was also the month of the Boi Mela or book fair. Nearby Bangla Academy's empty fields became filled with booksellers and poetry reciters and musicians from afternoon to night, adding exhilaration to our lives. As long as I lived on the Dhaka University campus, I tried to go to the Boi Mela every day, swinging by at least for a little while. I crossed over to the neighborhood para, took the back alley from there, and reached Bangla Academy in twenty minutes. I have no memory of ever going by myself. Even if I started out by myself, invariably I would run into someone going to the same location. All the bookstores of Dhaka and even from outside Dhaka had stalls at the Boi Mela. New books were routinely launched, though the launches were more informal than now, and the current system of morok ummochon, literally "opening the covers," did not exist at the time. Along with books, cassette tapes (it was the pre-CD era), posters, pottery, and snacks were available. Every year we waited to see how attractive they would make the temporary gate leading to Bangla Academy. Every evening throughout the month of February, music, poetry recitals, and discussions were held at the academy. Being at the Boi Mela made me feel at the center of all events, surrounded by strangers with whom I felt a close affinity as I fought through the crowd to enter a popular bookstall to lay my hands on a new book. Ah, the smell of a new book! The turning of pages, the sudden illuminating word that swept me off my feet, as I located a book I had long been looking for! Also the realization that I didn't have enough money, and the rationing of snacks for the sake of another book, walking away unfulfilled yet satiated to the brim.

Bangla Academy also hosted the Boishakhi Mela to celebrate the Bengali New Year in mid-April for the span of a week. Local artifacts, made of clay, paper, and metals, along with books and music, at that time in the form of cassette tapes, were available in abundance. Pohela Boishakh was a national holiday when people, instead of heading to their homes outside Dhaka, came to Dhaka or at least stayed back to enjoy the day of pomp and celebration. The weather was supposed to be mild at that time of the year, but after walking and being outside for hours it felt hot, though never hot enough for us to compromise on fashion, or to give up the discomforts of the yards-long sarees. The whole day was a big celebration, including a procession led by students from the Art Institute with exquisite papier-mâché masks and other symbols that had acquired epic proportions. The flowers of spring seemed lifeless in comparison to the waves of colors adorned by women, men, and children. Often the kalboishakhi, the summer storm, started on that very day, ending spring and heralding the beginning of summer. The kalboishakhi began with a speedy breeze cool enough to blow away the dominating heat, accompanied by huge and heavy raindrops, sudden and bristling, causing the unripe green mangoes and the dark purple jam to fall off the trees. The fallen fruits tasted so much better than the store-bought ones and there were plenty of huge trees around which everyone gathered to pick up the fruits. When I was growing up, the sense of proprietorship in Bangladesh accommodated neighbors, strangers, and even street children who joyfully lunged to pick up the fallen fruits, the kalboishakhi acting as the temporary benevolent equalizer.

While my Bengali identity was forming through Ekushe and Boishakhi Mela, my religious training was taking place haltingly. Often a religious teacher, an imam, whom we called hujoor, came to teach me Arabic in the early morning. The sleepy chants of "Alif, Ba, Ta, Sa" soon fizzled out as none of the teachers would stay for long. It took me a couple of years to finish learning the Arabic alphabet and "Ampara," the thirtieth chapter of the Quran with the shortest verses, as often the interruptions in study were longer than the period of study itself. A common madrassa soon started in the drivers' quarters over the rows of garages, where the rooms mostly remained empty as few university professors could afford cars. The elaborate two-room madrassa, segregating boys and girls, started with humming sounds in the afternoon, soon after school was over. I began with enthusiasm, struggling with my orna to keep my head covered, but after getting hit on the palm by a cane for improper pronunciation, I stopped going there. I was around eight at the time. The hujoor was rebuked when complaints piled up and he compromised by hitting only the boys while screaming at the girls. Gender discrimination sometimes worked in our favor!

On most mornings when there were no Arabic sessions there was a precious half hour when I went out with friends to collect flowers. There were a number of trees within the compound and it was common practice for kids to wake up early in the morning to gather the fallen flowers to make a garland, put them around neat little stems that peeped out from the grass, or take a fistful home or to a favorite teacher. We walked under the huge bokul tree and picked the small sweet yellow flowers and put them on long sticks plucked from the grass. The sweet smell of the fragrant tiny yellow bokul was everlasting, lingering on even after the flower turned brown, while the orange-stemmed bright white shiuli was prettier, more delicate, and had a shorter life. Often, my sister and I draped a garland over the picture of my dadi. Her only picture hung serenely from the wall, where she sat with her hands on her knees, flowers on the table to her side, silent and apprehensive. The contrast of the yellow and orange of the bokul and shiuli in the foggy morning against the backdrop of someone singing in the neighborhood, rushing and competing to gather more flowers, and hurrying to finish the garland to get ready for school are my associations with dadi. I have the same copy of her picture at home, but it feels incomplete without the soft touch of bokul mala that surrounded it all through my childhood.

My most important life lesson until that point was becoming an older sister and balancing affection and resentment toward someone who was five years younger and competing and catching up with me in various privileges. We had our ears pierced at the same time, me at ten and her at five, much to my chagrin. Nobody heeded my demand that "she should get her ears pierced five years *later!*" We often got the same amount of money as Eidi—close relatives giving little children money after being offered salaam for Eid—making me fume at the injustice of the age gap being eroded. My sister complains that all my life I struggled to keep up the entitlements of the older sister while she suffered, conveniently forgetting the embarrassments to which she subjected me. At a cultural function in the university quarters, I was reciting a poem with all the seriousness a seven-year-old could muster, when suddenly a two-year-old toddler jumped on stage, screaming "Apu, apu!" (big sister), excited at seeing me up there. What could I do? I stopped my recital and nudged her away with a slight smack on her chubby cheeks, embarrassed at the spectacle that was stripping away the seriousness of the event. Nausheen bawled like she had never been hit before. I paused and then continued my recital under the disapproving eyes of the audience. I could not believe that I was being criticized for my action, everyone exclaiming, "How could you slap that cute sister of yours?" while they sympathized with Nausheen.

"Your sister's head is split in half, blood is oozing out!" the gleeful shriek of the neighborhood kids once did stop my heartbeat as I ran along, only to find a trail of blood near the low table where Nausheen had hit her head, pretending to be blind in her solitary play. My dad, who rushed to the nearest Medical

College hospital where they stitched her head, was proud of her, claiming, "Nausheen never shed a single tear!" I remember my surge of affection, and showing off the blood marks and Nausheen's bandaged head to my playmates. Nausheen also bestowed upon me the authority of the elder sister and basking in that glory I made decisions as to who could pick her up and squish her, only to be overridden by her ayah. My mom sided with the ayah, telling me to listen to her, as she tried to protect Nausheen from a gang of my friends who carelessly lifted her, squeezed her, and then unceremoniously dropped her to rush toward the next game on the playground. I could exercise some of my sisterly duties when she started school, since we both went to Udayan Bidyalaya, which shared a common wall with our compound. I took her tiffin and made sure that she ate the sandwiches or the boiled potatoes and peas or the runny half-boiled eggs properly. At school, she often forgot her drawing book or some exercise book, and begged me, "Please, please, please, I only need one taka to buy a new drawing book!" That precious one taka was my tiffin money. With a sigh and a few strong words, I handed over my one taka and she started running to the small store at the end of the school, accessible to us through a narrow lane where only one person could walk comfortably over the slabs covering the sewage drain.

Just as my Bengali and religious teachings combated in my formation, the very different parenting techniques of my mom and dad constantly confused me and my sister. My dad, a professor of international relations at Dhaka University, lived in his own world and I understood early on that he was not an efficient navigator of the real world. He was oblivious to our needs and wants, his academic pursuits looming larger than anything else. My mom had inherited not only her deep religious beliefs but also a gregarious personality from her parents. The only sister among her four brothers (two sisters died in infancy before she was born), she was pampered and often acted as the third parent to her younger brothers, tutoring and disciplining them. Since her parents moved back and forth between Kolkata and Dhaka, often leaving her for a couple of months to finish her school year, she was also very independent, traveling by herself between Kolkata and Dhaka, a rarity for a young girl in those days. She was always immaculately dressed, every object from the tip on her forehead to her shoes matching perfectly, yet she never missed a prayer. The system of arranged marriage united my father and mother through a common acquaintance who knew my dad's aunt, but I have never seen two people more poles apart. My sister and I thank our lucky stars that our parents did not coordinate their messages, which would have deprived us of the ability to draw from two very different models and to tolerate the parts we ended up rejecting.

"Why are you wasting your precious time reading storybooks? You should learn ten new words from the dictionary each day," my dad would say to us a little louder than necessary, so that my mom, lounging with her own book of fiction before her afternoon nap, could hear. A stellar student, she paid little attention to scholarly pursuits after publishing her solitary book *Muslim Politics in Bengal: A Study of the Krishak Praja Party and the Elections of 1937*, while my dad was always sitting at his desk on the balcony or at the dining table with a stack of books and articles, working on a paper, and taking off his spectacles to concentrate. My mom carried my sister's bike, a novelty for girls in those days (though not any more), up and down the stairs, while my dad averted physical strain of any kind, such as carrying luggage, getting shots from the doctor, or even pouring water from a heavy jug. If anything went wrong at home, such as the fuse blowing out, something needing to be hammered, or an electronic device that had quit working, it was always my mom who rose to the task, never my dad.

"Isn't it nine o'clock yet?" my dad would ask, wandering into the living room to catch the news while we took a break from our regular viewing. I grew up mostly watching the single channel that was available, Bangladesh Television. While my dad prodded us to limit our television viewing, my mom would show us her notebook which contained a list of almost three hundred movies, along with notes on actors, actresses, music directors, and her brief analyses, movies she had seen in Kolkata as a teenager. As movies in Bangladesh were of poor quality and my dad was unwilling to accompany her, she compensated by watching television diligently, staying awake until Bangladesh Television went dark, while we were only allowed an hour of television each night. My dad wandered in, oblivious to what we were watching, and tried to engage us with questions like, "Do you think the election will take place?" My dad has always been bored to death in America, while my mom excitedly visits the mall, talks to strangers (I once found her debating the Jehovah's Witnesses for over an hour), surfs the channels, and finds shows like , and Murder, *She Wrote,* shows I never knew were still on as reruns. Nausheen, now a psychologist in the U.S. Navy, and I often wonder about our parents who were diametrically different, one temperamental, outgoing, and social, the other serious and philosophical, only their love and concern for us binding them together.

Going out to a friend's place invoked countless questions from my dad, such as "Where are you going?" or "With whom are you going?" or "When are you coming back?" which irritated even my mom. I had to wait until my mid-twenties when I came to Canada to listen to my first uninterrupted album. In all fairness, though, he limited his agonizing to annoyingly long trails of questions, rather than any actions to constrict the freedom we enjoyed which was more than the average household's in Dhaka. Although he regarded storybooks as a waste of time, it was he who took me to the British Council and paid for my first library card. He urged me to use the privilege of library books for educational and developmental purposes, though I used the library for pleasure reading and peeking into adult books, too scared to try to borrow them on my own.

My mother was a strict disciplinarian, having had long years of practice managing, scolding, and hitting her younger brothers, who were naughty kids. She followed that model assiduously with us, demanding, "Where did you leave the twenty points? Why is it only eighty out of a hundred?" amid occasional beatings, slappings, and smackings with the handy ruler, which was not uncommon at the time, not only at home but occasionally at school as well. My dad, on the other hand, rarely scolded us. The only time I was slapped by him was when I tore a piece of paper from the exams he was grading and used it to make a boat to sail in the drain overflowing with the monsoon rain. Mostly he tried to persuade me to be a good girl, comparing me to "Dilruba," his lost daughter who was exemplary in everything: Dilruba always got hundred out of hundred in every subject, never cried, never watched television, and ate everything placed in front of her. I longed to be like Dilruba and had prodigious fantasies of searching for her, finding her, and one day being reunited. She had become so real to me that it broke my heart (I was around seven) when my dad casually laughed and admitted that Dilruba had been a figment of his imagination.

"Tell us a story!" we begged when electricity went off in the evenings and we played with our shadows on the wall. My mom obliged, reciting stories from her childhood, her favorite Agatha Christie mysteries, or tales of historical characters if she was in the middle of class preparation. Emperor Humayun, who allowed the throne to the water-bearer for a day as a reward for saving his life, became human to us rather than the failed king who lost his kingdom. We could see the young Akbar fleeing from town to town in disguise, taking help from the common people, and understood what compelled him to look for a new religion to bring people together. We could hear the merciless teasing of Napoleon by his playmates, the elite in Delhi gossiping about Razia Sultana, the only woman to ascend to the throne of Delhi, and the seething resentment of Aurangzeb toward his father for favoring his elder brother; all these characters became sympathetic and vulnerable in my mom's stories. I have been told by her former students that she was a wonderful teacher. When my sister went to the U.S., for years and years my mom used to write her each day and mail a week's worth of writing at a time as she wanted Nausheen to vicariously experience our everyday life. I awaited her letters to me in Canada and in Cleveland, the small rounded alphabets saying so much even if they didn't contain any news. Even her emails feel like flash fiction, a description of an event or a person I have no idea about, yet sparking my curiosity. My dad wrote at most ten letters to me in his life, all very formal, practical, and full of advice. Their letters contain so much of the contrast of their personalities.

My dad perfectly fit the prototype of the absent-minded professor. He had a history of not only losing keys, money, and other things, but interestingly, also of recovering them. I was once with him on our way to Motijheel, Dhaka's downtown, when he left behind the edited version of an article on which he had worked for days. Amazingly, we got the same scooter on our way back, the article lying in the corner of the seat! But everything pales in comparison to his adventure when he lost the only copy of his PhD thesis. He did his PhD at Jawaharlal Nehru University in Delhi from 1979 to 1984 and he used to come to Dhaka every few months, ostensibly for data collection, but I suspect more from the burning desire to see us. He took the Rajdhani Express from Delhi to Kolkata and then the bus from the border. He had started his program in 1979 and was typing his dissertation at the time. This event took place in 1981. As he got out of the train in Kolkata, a coolie came and took his bag with the only copy of his dissertation and disappeared into the crowd. It was actually a technique of theft. I cannot imagine what my dad must have experienced. He went through the formalities of reporting the crime. Both the station master and the police told him to consider his baggage lost and to move on. It was considered a common petty theft and would not garner much attention. He kept pestering them, staying at the station for a week, building relationships with the police, the station manager, and even the coolie sardar, begging them that he needed only the bunch of papers from his luggage; not only was he ready to forego his luggage, but he would also pay for the papers. He thought that his life had ended and he could bear to retreat neither to Delhi nor to Dhaka without the dissertation. At last, a police officer took pity on him and escorted him to a place where materials recovered from theft were kept. My dad speaks of a labyrinth leading to a cavernous room where suitcases and bags of every shape and color were heaped in piles, luggage that would likely never end up with the proper owners. My dad roamed the large room and worked his way through the narrow spaces between the piles and found his suitcase. He discovered everything intact and was about to leave with only his dissertation when the officer told him that he could take back the whole suitcase. Losing luggage at Howrah Station to theft is common enough, but finding it happens perhaps only once in a blue moon. My dad's habit of making a photocopy of every document must have started from that event.

All the experiences of recovering lost or stolen articles could not cure my dad's lifelong fear of theft. He also told us an improbable story about his bag being stolen from a railway car on his way to Rajshahi University where he taught for a year after coming back from Holland upon finishing his master's. He provided a list of things that were in his bag when he lodged the complaint with the station master. The thief was caught within the space of a couple of stations as he had taken out the clothes that belonged to my dad and put them on. He was wearing the tie inside out, and the TT (ticket checker) reported him. For all his worries about theft, his actual experiences were positive ones. Most of the trouble was caused by his absent-mindedness when he misplaced important documents. The items he lost or thought he had lost, leading to frantic searches, included not only numerous books every couple of weeks (sometimes lost, sometimes found), but also my SSC certificate (thankfully only misplaced) and his green card (lost in transit as it was in a book he lost in Malaysia).

"Mehnaaz, let's walk for a little bit," he would say, and I would accompany him to the university, quibbling about politics. Our walk to the university library or the adjacent British Council library could easily end in calamity as my dad, who never used a wallet and kept the house key inserted in books, often realized that he had returned the book which contained the key. The Dhaka University librarian knew it every time he saw my father return within half an hour of turning in a book, as silently smiling he patted the pile of books waiting to be processed. At the British Council library, however, there was a book drop and instead of neat piles we encountered jumbles of books as the librarian allowed us to go in and look for the books. They also processed books much faster, so if the loss of the key was not discovered within a couple of hours the book was already reshelved, making it harder for us to look for it. In those cases, we had to wait for my mom to come back in the late afternoon to access the master bedroom. The chabiwala (locksmith) always welcomed the sight of us, which irritated my mother. Once, when my mom was chiding my dad in front of him, he interjected that my dad was such a nice man. My mom's response was, "Yes, you would say that. He [meaning my dad] has helped your business so much!"

I remember most things being locked away when we were growing up and a bunch of keys changing hands several times a day. Maybe it was a characteristic of the culture of poverty and being on guard against servants rolled together. Once I lost the bunch that had keys to every lock belonging to us. It was just before my all-important board exam for the tenth grade, and the timing saved me. It is still a mystery how I managed to lose that big and heavy bunch without leaving the house. My parents had to replace every lock and key. Years later, I found a bunch of old locks in my mom's closet and was told that these were the very locks whose keys I had lost twenty years ago. The nonfunctional locks had been preserved during two moves, in case the keys might be found some day. Such is the power of hope! I miss those old heavy locks and keys that made one feel secure. I remember the metallic touch being cool and soothing and wondering about the work of locksmiths. Walking for miles and miles in the blazing sun or unexpected rain was no doubt a difficult life, but the ringing of various metal keys on a huge wire and the occasional cry of talachabi, meaning lock and key, filled my childhood with the sounds of adventure, the quest undertaken by the locksmith and the cobbler who dared to lurk in all parts of the city.

With my mom, we went out shopping, visited the tailor (most of our clothes were custom-made), or watched a natok (Bengali theater) at Baily Road. Once there was an Indian Bangla movie show during the flood of 1988 which submerged the urban areas when my cousin Munmun apa was visiting. Determined to show her a good time and not be deterred by the flood, we all piled into a rickshaw to go to Ananda Cinema Hall, a considerable distance from our university quarters, in knee-deep water. The rickshaw had to stop near an elevated island dividing the street where we hopped off and balanced ourselves on pieces of wood and brick to cross the nearly empty streets (most people were not mad enough to venture out on the flooded streets) to reach the cinema hall. I will always remember our laughter after first being careful, then giving in to the water surrounding us, watching the movie in soaked slacks, and standing for ages before a rickshaw puller agreed to take us back with the promise of double fare.

Every couple of months, I found myself stepping into our living room with rearranged furniture, my mom sweating and energized after her solitary effort. My mom also made fanciful travel plans, of which only a small proportion were ever realized. As luck would have it, I often got sick before major events—like coming down with jaundice before a family vacation to Chittagong—forcing her to change plans. She did not take to these incidents kindly and did not act as the stereotypical Bengali mom, patiently sitting beside the child's sickbed. Most of my memories of sickness are being stricken with guilt and scolded, "Why are you so weak? Why do you have to get sick just before vacation? You were fine all year round!" Both Nausheen and I had motion sickness, which, according to my mother, was a lowly problem that irked her to no end. My headaches, which started around the age of ten, were such a source of agitation to her that I often did not mention them. Nausheen and I both suffered from measles and mumps, and had to go through appendectomy as well. The day Nausheen recovered from measles and was released from quarantine, we danced with joy to celebrate, but the next day I promptly fell ill and was diagnosed with measles. My mother lamented her strategy of keeping us apart, saying, "It would have been so much better if you two had been sick at the same time!" We also got mumps one after another, upsetting my mom. We both had appendectomy in our mid-teens. Mine was the first notable surgery in the family. I enjoyed every ounce of attention and the exaggerated worries of my dad, as he refused to sign the necessary paperwork giving the doctors permission for the surgery. Five or six years later, when Nausheen went through the same procedure, it had lost the aura of apprehension.

We might have been in the habit of visiting our relatives and friends all over Dhaka, but trips outside Dhaka, except to our village home, were rare. Both my mom's older brothers, and my dad's younger brother, Alam chacha or chhoto chacha, lived in Chittagong, less than two hundred miles away, but I went to Chittagong only four or five times. My dad's elder brother, Monu chacha or boro chacha, was a government magistrate and they moved every couple of years to new cities like Rajendropur or Noakhali. We made many plans to visit them, but none of these plans ever came to pass. Boro chacha had six children, Rima, Rupa, Ruchi, Ria, Ripon, and Riko, and chhoto chacha three, Liza, Niaz, and Lita, but I never got to meet them more than once or twice a year when I was growing up. Eventually, both my uncles moved and settled in Dhaka, but I only got to see my cousins fleetingly. My dad's youngest sister, Daisy, had a daughter, Runa, around my age, but they went to Libya when I was in class four, coming back four or five years later and making it awkward for us to resume our friendship. I came to acknowledge Runa as a friend later, in our late teens, though I have happy memories of playing with her as a child. The only place filled with cousins that we frequented was at my boro phuppi, my dad's eldest sister, who was not much older than him but because she had been married at fifteen her ten children were much older than me.

I have more memories of Tanya and Zafreen, second cousins of my age who were my playmates. Much later, at my in-laws' place, I realized that the lack of constant interaction with close relatives had left me unprepared for the intricacies of life in a joint family setting. Neither my mother nor my nani had had a mother-in-law so I inherited no horror stories of gender injustice. Because almost all my uncles and aunts from both parts of the family lived outside Dhaka, our interactions were mainly pleasant; even if there were disagreements, they never had the time and scope to germinate into full-blown family conflicts of the type so common in Bangladesh.

Another gaping hole because of the absence of cousins or an elder sister was that I had no one to approach other than my friends about information regarding sex. The level of knowledge of my friends was as shallow as mine and my mother remained tight-lipped and pretended that no such issue existed. My sexual knowledge came mainly from the maidservants. My mother did not explain properly what a period was even when I had one. I had more accurate information from one of my friends and when I asked my mom for further clarification, she insisted that it was all lies. I was eleven years old when she vehemently denied my hushed questions, the answers to which were of course revealed to me pretty soon. Even then there was no proper explanation and everything was focused on how shameful the event was and how I had to hide it at all costs from the rest of the world.

The person to whom I owe immense gratitude for teaching me about periods, sex, and childbirth without any confusion was Shorupa, the young girl who worked for us. Her name was really Sharifa, but she had changed it to Shorupa. Dark and always smiling, she used to tell me wonderful stories of her three sisters, one who was abducted by a dacoit and had to marry him, one who was beautiful and had to be hidden to make sure no marriage proposals came for her before her elder sisters, and one who was going to school and facing insurmountable obstacles. Her village, near Manikganj, less than a hundred miles from Dhaka, seemed to be in another world. I pleaded with her in the quiet afternoons while my parents were taking a nap to resolve the confusing issues of sex, love, and relationships, and she obliged, sharing stories of her own affair with a helper at a street stall who made dalpuri. My sister and I also demanded "normal" stories from her every night and in the half-dark room, lit only by the illumination on the balcony, her yellow and blue translucent saree glowing, she took us to another dimension. I don't know the proportion of truth and exaggeration and pure fantasy in her stories, but I do know that her power of imagination served me and my sister well.

All of the young girls who worked at our house, often for a couple of years, had been denied the opportunity to go to school. We started teaching them enthusiastically but the excitement on both sides faded after they learnt to sign their names, and often they left to get married. Kamala, the girl who stayed at our place the longest, more than twelve years, had just finished learning to write her name when her mother asked us to teach her Arabic. My mother took over, but those sessions did not go far as both my mother and Kamala preferred taking naps in the afternoon and watching television over reciting "alif, ba, ta, sa." Kamala was not too enthusiastic about Bengali, and even slower in Arabic, but she could sing any tune she heard. Her lifelong wish was to own a radio, but when granted this wish by my uncles she moved on to a cassette player, and used to take care of it like a baby. Now she is married with her own two daughters, Sonia and Tanya, who are going to school. Kamala has had a stable and secure life, but all her desires for music, movies, and other enjoyments have had to be relegated to the background.

Countless girls and women have worked at our place over the years. We, or at least I, never thought twice about ordering them around. My mom had a reputation of providing well for the maids, better than the average household, and somehow this justified our demands of asking them to bring us a book or a glass of water any time of the day or night. My mother gave Kamala time off one afternoon each week until late evening, much to the annoyance of our neighbors as this set a bad example. My father asked us and the maids for a glass of water, standing right in front of the water pitcher and the glass. My mother scolded Kamala as liberally as she scolded us. With Kamala, because of her long presence, issues assumed a twisted longevity. She had been married at a very young age, barely thirteen, and her mother sold off their small parcel of land to give the money to her husband to start a shop, with which he promptly disappeared within a month of marriage, never to be heard from again. We were all sympathetic toward her quest to find a husband the second time around, but dealing with her pent-up frustration and fits of outbursts was not easy on any of us. A number of young men—chauffeurs, guards, brothers-in-law of other maids—tried to woo fair Kamala, who had a way with words, but all backed off from proposing marriage. The stigma of getting married to a girl who worked as a maid, that too a divorced woman, was too strong, though Kamala was sought after for flirting and dates. Kamala was not looking for dates; all she craved for was a respectable marriage. But her quest landed her in a quandary, whether to trust a person enough to get involved and shun other suitors, or to go on looking for a husband. The situation was made more chaotic by the fact that each of these suitors promised marriage, but none followed through. I remember hearing her stories of betrayal and secretly being grateful for my class privileges.

I also remember Hasina, dark and buck-toothed with a pleasant smile, who worked at my nani's house and who told me the story of her divorce, her policeman husband turning vicious as soon as he put on his uniform and becoming very loving when he took it off. She kept insisting, "It was the uniform! He used to change as soon as he wore it." There was Saleha, our cook from Faridpur, who used to smoke bidi (a cheaper version of the local handmade cigarette), much to our surprise and my mother's disapproval. But no one was like Shorupa. I don't remember if she was with us for a long time or not. She continued visiting even when she no longer worked for us. She made us pitha, a sweet cake-like dessert, and I particularly remember the one that involved leaves from the jackfruit tree. There was a semi-liquid concoction of flour and sugar with which she drew designs on the leaves. When it thickened, the leaves were placed in a sieve over a pot of boiling water and the steam separated the pitha from the leaves. I had forgotten about all this, until a few years ago, at a traditional Mexican cookout, the making of tamales made me remember those occasions when I was given the duty to clean the leaves from the jackfruit tree and lightly brush them with oil. Shorupa and Saleha made achar, or pickle, competing with each other and goading us, "Which one is better? You have to tell us the truth!" We complied, depending on whom we liked more at the time, reserving the right to swiftly change our minds. Now I am amazed at how these women, who all had histories of misfortune which purged them from their villages and made them come to work at the homes of strangers, held on to their humor, self-respect, and conviction knowing the stark options staring at them.

Shorupa, indeed, had a tragic end to her life. She had stopped working for us when I was around ten and later became the caretaker of my ailing nani. After my nani died, she worked somewhere else but visited us every now and then. She showed up one day, when I was around seventeen, wanting to stay for the night and crying a lot. No amount of urging and coaxing from me or my mother would convince her to divulge her secret sorrows. She used to keep her savings in my mother's safekeeping and she wanted the money back. She went to her village, only to come back within a couple of weeks, claiming to be very sick. We took her to a doctor and discovered that she had become dangerously anemic. She had no explanation of her deterioration in just a few weeks. She fainted the next day and in the hospital it was revealed that she was suffering from a botched abortion. The doctors needed more information, which she steadfastly refused to provide, denying the abortion all the while. She needed blood, which she got, but her infection had spread and after two weeks in the hospital she was given medication with the dire prognosis of suffering for the rest of her life. She did not suffer much, as she died within a week of her release in her village home. What is ironic is that safe and cheap abortion was and still remains accessible to girls and women almost everywhere in Bangladesh. Shorupa was deterred from getting proper aid not because of the lack of access but because of her sense of social shame.

I remember her tears, my helplessness, and her obstinate stance with the doctors all too well, but mostly I remember her laughter, my badgering regarding information about sex, and her whispering back invaluable information after extracting multiple promises never to tell my mother. She was ten to twelve years older than me, and filled my yearning for an elder sister or unavailable cousins. When I reflect now, I am both astonished and grateful at how she explained sex, male-female relationships, and childbirth with such candor and accuracy, careful to use language fit for a nine or ten year old to easily understand and digest.

In a twist of poetic justice, it is very difficult to find maids in Dhaka these days as they prefer to work in the garment industry, working harder but earning more, and enjoying more freedom than being at someone's beck and call for twenty-four hours a day. Mukta, the very young girl who stays at our house now—forced to be a maid after her parents divorced and her relatives could not offer a place safe enough for a fourteen-year-old—had studied up to class four. Now she has the opportunity to continue her studies in return for her labor. Although her level of education at the village school was quite weak, she still caught up with the public school standard. If this anecdotal example is a reflection of changes in academic standards, that in itself is revolutionary. I suspect exposure through television, movies, and technology has played a pivotal role in bringing Mukta on the same page as her peers going to better schools and growing up in better socio-economic conditions.

Captivity

My life at the Issa Khan Road university quarters stopped abruptly when I was in class seven as I had to give up my friends, playground, and my freedom to move to my grandparents' house on College Street when my father left for Delhi for his PhD. This move lasted for four long years, years that were routine, dull, and insipid in comparison to living in the university para. My sister and I vehemently resisted the move but for tortuous reasons (safety, convenience, savings, and the avoidance of daily chores, all jumbled together in my mom's fantasy of going back to her youth by living in her old home), we had to make the move. As our furniture was loaded on trucks and some on thelagari (pushcarts), my sister shed tears for our lost world. Our world did indeed shrink with that move. The bedroom, where everything was always prim and proper, the study, where we propped up toys and books on the guest bed and played loudly, the living room, where we watched television or entertained guests, and our balcony which had witnessed the transformation of two babies to toddlers and then to young girls of twelve and seven, along with their imaginary friends, their fantasies, their contentment in the lazy afternoons, and their tears of pain over unfair adults, all had to be left behind.

The single room we all stayed in at our grandparents' house was quite big, in the middle of the house, and flanked by two large windows and four doors connecting it to two balconies, the living room, and another bedroom through a bathroom, which meant that everyone was always crossing through that room. Except for our bed, tables, and almirahs, the rest of our stuff was in a room above the garage, jam-packed and locked. My mother unlocked it once a month to dust and to make sure that everything was all right. These became special days as my sister and I affectionately touched our things—the dining table, toys, boxes—longing to have our independent life back. Our world retreated to that one room, congested by a bed, two tables and chairs, a dressing table, and two almirahs. If I sat at my desk and moved the chair, it touched the bed. Every time anyone wanted to pass through that room—my nana or nani to go to the living room or dining area, the maidservant looking for my nani, anyone who wanted to make a phone call or people rushing to take a call as the only phone was in my nana-nani's bedroom—I had to get up and pull my chair aside to let that person pass. Studying at the dining table was not an option as the television was always on in the living area of the same room.

The sofas in the living room were protected with covers and we were prodded to sit on the old ones rather than the springy new ones that we preferred. I remember my nani being overprotective of her furniture, her dishes, and all her stuff, a trait I found overbearing. Now I wonder if it was a displaced projection of her care for her children who were mostly away, in Chittagong, in America, outside the home almost all the time. Her face and demeanor completely changed when my uncles were visiting. We looked forward to the yearly visit of my uncle and his family from Chittagong and the rare visits from the uncles in the U.S.

The drab routine of lunch, dinner, and namaz, or daily prayers, fully occupied my grandparents' life. There was nothing to do but to stay cooped up in the house after school. I was not as lucky as Nausheen who found a friend among the neighbors. My friends in the neighborhood, Muna, Lara, and Shumi, kept moving to new places. We tried playing badminton on the roof but nani dissuaded us by saying, "The roof will fall apart with all that jumping!"

A couple of hours of television—between maghrib and isha prayers, that is, between sunset and dinner—was our only entertainment. I remember nana and nani sitting on the long sofa, my uncle sitting sideways on the smaller one closest to the television, his legs up on the arms of the sofa, my mother on another small sofa, and my sister and I on the carpet, while the new sofa remained unsullied, and the hired help sat on the edge of the carpet, maintaining a safe distance from us. I grew up watching many American television shows, but usually I got to watch them several years after they were released in America. *Dallas* was the first serial shown in Bangladesh while it was being shown in America. Nani, however, knew who had shot JR as she had watched it while visiting my uncles in the U.S., and just as we were about to watch the most suspenseful serial of the day, she nonchalantly revealed the killer to us. I still remember the dismay and crushed look on chhotu's face!

Books became the only solace of my life in captivity. I had already raided my uncles' treasure trove of comic books: , and a horde of Western comics that were kept under lock and key. I remember several classics like Somerset Maugham, along with more pedestrian fare like Harold Robbins and James Hadley

Chase, in my uncle's collection. My nana loved and collected Perry Mason and P. G. Wodehouse. My mother's collection of Agatha Christie and her huge stockpile of Bengali literature, which were deemed unsuitable for my age, were at last in the bookshelves on the balcony. I had to read most books on the sly by inserting them within a textbook. I became quite reckless and finished her whole stack and when after my SSC my mother formally gave me permission to read her books, there wasn't a single book I had left unread. Once the taboo was lifted, all the adult books became vapid. Except for being fascinated by the pace and the sex, and the thrill of hiding the book within the cover of an accepted book, these books left little mark on me, except for one. There was a book on Islam which had detailed descriptions of following religious edicts in everyday life, including sexual encounters between husbands and wives. Written in direct, crude, and clinical language, it provided the first exposure to porn in our very limited world. Later I found out that for many of my friends this very book had been their first stop for sexual knowledge as it had been for me.

How I longed for a space of my own! I wished I could have my own corner on the balcony, where I could sit for hours without being asked hundreds of questions, and my own bed in my own room where I could lie down with a book undisturbed. My mother assigned me a drawer in a huge squat white cupboard sitting on the balcony and it soon became crammed with a diary, some books, some cards, bits and pieces of wrapping paper I had saved, nice pencils, pens, stickers, and money hidden in small boxes or purses, all of it filling the drawer to the brim so that I had to lift it up a little to open it. How can you fit a teenager's life in a single drawer? The contents started spilling over in notebooks with a myriad of unfinished stories along with a few complete ones.

I missed the easy energetic spirit of the campus as a more serious religious fervor set the tone for our lives. My mom had always prayed regularly four times a day (skipping the early morning fajr prayer as she used to prioritize sleep, at least then), but instead of being the only one in the household who was praying, now she was with the majority, and soon my sister and I started praying regularly as well. My dad only went for the Friday noon prayer, jumma namaz, which was for him more of a social gathering like the Sunday Mass. He also attended the two Eid prayers, which again were more cultural and festive events where religion took the backstage. I never knew my mom to miss fasting, but for my dad, who drinks water every hour, fasting was pure torture. Like kids, he used to fast only once, on the twenty-seventh of Ramazan, the most auspicious day, and I suspect only to be able to claim that he had fasted without divulging details. At nanabari my nana, nani, mom, and chhotu read the Quran diligently all through the holy month of Ramazan. I was eager to fast, because getting up in the middle of the night to have sehri, receiving special treatment during iftar, and feeling the proud swell of my chest at stepping into the grown-up world were all hard to resist, even if it meant giving up food and drink from sunrise to sunset. Although sticking to prayer was hard and one had to have a lot of discipline, I felt like an outlier as everyone else said their prayers as soon as the azan, or the call for prayers, was heard. The mosque was across the street, and it was impossible to miss the high-pitched azan five times a day.

It was the azan which established the rhythm of our lives. We had lunch after zohr prayers, tea after asr prayers, and dinner after isha prayers. I don't remember being told to pray, but in an environment where everyone, including my cricket-playing uncle, prayed regularly, it made sense to join the group. The positive reinforcement my grandparents bestowed on us was also unparalleled. If we prayed, especially my sister, nana would bring home jilapi, the saccharine-sweet syrupy orange dessert, on his way home from the mosque. Jilapi is my strongest association with namaz, to this day.

We started with maghrib prayers and soon were praying four times a day consistently. We were never coerced and were allowed to sleep through the early morning fajr prayer. My mom was not as enthusiastic about us fasting as she was about us saying our prayers, but she relented to our demands. When my sister and I fasted, festive iftar dishes were prepared for us and we got exceptional treatment indeed. My only duty during Ramazan was to make lemonade for the whole household. I remember the huge white tin bowl with faint red edges into which I poured sugar and squeezed lemons, trying to balance the sweet and sour taste which was so refreshing after a day of fasting. I made a big fuss if I were fasting and not able to taste it. I would only put a drop in my mouth and then spit it out as I wouldn't swallow it. Sehri and iftar became enjoyable events. The nightlong prayers during Shab-e-Barat, when everyone's fate is being rewritten and prayers provide the opportunity once a year to nudge it in a desirable direction, were joyful as well. We competed to stay awake and bragged about the number of rakats of namaz we had prayed.

Horrified that we had yet to finish the Quran, nana found a religious teacher who instructed us while everyone was taking a siesta in the afternoon. Finally, in class nine, I finished the Quran, quite late in life; there was a milad in my honor, and my grandparents and mom were proud of me. It must have been the influence of the place, because after we left their house, my sister's Quran lessons stopped and she never finished it. And after that pride-filled grand ending, I have never opened a page of the Quran. The way we were taught to read the holy book was a waste of time and energy. I learnt the alphabet and could read the Quran without understanding a single word. I developed no curiosity, no interest, and no identification with the Quran all through the years-long quest to grasp it. I had to learn a bit of Arabic for my religious studies exam in the SSC, which involved knowing the meaning and context of parts of the Quran and hadith. Finishing the Quran did not help me even in those instances. It seemed like everyone had to go through the meaningless suffering and I did my time as well. Now when Jim, my all-white American colleague, takes Arabic language classes and brags about his Arabic, I regret spending so much time and getting nothing out of it. Even our prayers, meaning my sister's and mine, ceased after we came back to the university quarters after my father returned from Delhi, at first because I was busy preparing for the SSC exam, but after that because neither my sister nor I felt like it. What I remember more are the hadith, which my grandfather used to share before dinner.

Like saying grace before dinner, my nana recited guidance and stories from Prophet Muhammad's life, generally known as hadith, although only a small proportion are authentic. The rest are feel-good stories or folklore about kindness, justice, and respect for parents, elders, and other religions. The books were cheap and printed on newsprint, with countless grammatical errors. There were stories about Jesus and Moses, the Jesus stories being monotonous with afflicted men and women in pain, in contrast to the colorful Moses stories which were filled with greed, war, animosity, and, of course, magic. The only controversy I remember is regarding gender equality when my sister, my mom, and I raised questions about the validity of obeying the husband. To his credit, my grandfather backed down and laughed at his defeat as the three of us kept mounting our challenges. I remember being upset about the fact that during akika, the naming ceremony, for a boy the ritual was to sacrifice two goats but for a girl it was only one, and nana just smiled shyly and said that girls were helpful to their parents from the very beginning. Instead of trying to win the argument, he conceded, making sure that the disagreement petered out.

The version of religion I grew up with was not at all militant, but a much milder interpretation that focused on social justice, like zakat, which requires giving away two and a half percent of one's savings (measured by money in the bank and gold ornaments) to the poor every year. Zakat is defined not as voluntary charity, but as an obligation on the part of the giver. However mild the version of religion, it never properly blended in with Bengali culture. My mother's family, including all my uncles, carried an aversion toward Bengali names. My cousin Munmun apa named her son Ekushe (the "twenty-first" in Bengali) as he was born on 21 or Ekushe February, our Language Day. Her dad, my eldest uncle, had died in an untimely manner, never getting to see Ekushe or his other grandchildren. I would have loved to see his face if he had to digest a name like Ekushe!

I had only seen my nana with a beard and a black spot on his forehead from regular prayers, always getting ready for the next one. My mom's stories about her handsome dad, going to watch every cricket match with tiffin carriers filled with paratha and meat, taking in every new movie that came out, and having musical gatherings from time to time at their home, remained legends that did not match the person I knew as my nana. I wish I had asked him about his transformation when he was alive. I don't think nana regretted any of his swashbuckling past; rather, he relished talking about his music, movie, and Kolkata days. He did watch movies and listen to music with interest until the very end. Yet this was the same person who went to the mosque to stay there for forty days during Ramazan and who visited the urban outskirts and rural areas on tabligh missions to preach the proper form of Islam. I wish I could go back in time and ask him how he ever reconciled the two very different sides of him. My guess is that he didn't. A large and very significant part of his life remained outside the purview of his chosen philosophy, and that was the part my mother and her brothers reminisced about.

Islam in Bangladesh, as in other parts of the subcontinent, both clashed and melded with the local culture. The irritating question of whether one is a Bengali first or a Muslim first remains a haunting question for our national identity. I heaved a sigh of relief in the mid-nineties after I came to North America where both seemed unproblematic, but of course 9/11 and the militant nationalism and attack on multiculturalism that followed it clouded the question of identity in a way that is much more troublesome than theoretical debates. I now view ambiguity, porousness, and confusion in national identity as positive signs in a society, because a society that allows space for inconsistencies is a more tolerant society. The society I grew up in was largely Muslim, and although you heard the azan five times a day, you also celebrated a number of cultural rituals not rooted in religion, such as Pohela Boishakh, the first day of the Bengali calendar, or gaye holud, the ritual before the wedding day, with equal zest and fanfare. Amartya Sen informs us that the Bengali calendar was derived during Emperor Akbar's time, combining solar and lunar calculations, and compressing Islamic and Sanskrit calendars. Maybe therein lies the core of Bengali identity: it is an amalgamation of seemingly contradicting forces, with towering figures like Tagore who occasionally transcend opposing currents by taming them with poetry, music, spirituality, and philosophy binding Bengalis across national boundaries.

My nana was a practicing Muslim in every possible way, and he was comfortable conversing in Urdu, but he wrote poems in Bengali. I, however, used to become upset when he talked to Bihari refugees in Urdu. The Bihari refugees were the people who had migrated to then East Pakistan and sided with West Pakistan during the Liberation War, only to be left behind in Bangladesh and treated as treasonous non-citizens. They remained stateless, caught in the political drama of partition and liberation, and only very recently got Bangladeshi citizenship. A substantial number of them still want to reach the promised land of Pakistan, but they remain mostly segregated, spatially and culturally, stuck in Bangladesh. Nana had a close friend in Kolkata, Malati Ghosh, whom we always visited whenever we went to Kolkata. I remember the black bordered invitation for his sraddho (the Hindu ritual for death) that came in the mail, my nana murmuring barely audibly, "I will never get to see him again!"

My guess is that for my nana, religious rituals replaced his violin, music, and poetry, and the mosque replaced his adda with card-playing friends. Replacing cultural activities with religious rituals may have been his choice and not so problematic for him, but it had serious consequences for my nani. She started forgetting things in my early teens. At first it was misplacing keys or important papers or money, but soon it started getting worse and the doctors, both in Dhaka and in America, gave her medication for early dementia, medication that made her irritable, sleepy, and disassociated. She started forgetting suras, the verses, needed to say her prayers. Since this was associated with religion, she became anxious and guilty and fearful. Instead of calming her fears, my nana appointed a lady who taught her the suras all over again, which was useless as her memory was rapidly failing. She needed someone to stand by her while she said her prayers. My uncle, my mom, my sister, my cousin, and I, we all took turns assisting her. Standing in the namaz she suddenly stopped and faltered, waiting to take the cue from the person helping her. I would whisper, "Iyya kana budu," and she remembered that sura again, only to stop at the next sura. It became a burden to be with her and say every verse so that she could repeat it five times a day. On top of it, she was in constant agony as to whether or not she had said her prayers. The rational and humane option would have been to persuade her to stop it. How insecure she must have felt during those prayers! My mother pleaded with my nana, "Why is it not Allah's will that she has forgotten her prayers?" but he responded, "We go to the doctor when we are sick. She has to try to say her prayers, the rest is Allah's will."

In a culture where expressions of affection between couples are subtle and private, I remember the tender glances when nani used to call, "Ogo shunchho?" (Hey, are you listening?), not uttering her husband's name. Having been married at fifteen, she started having babies when she was seventeen. Five of her eight children lived. Nani used to tell us stories about when she was a tomboy and stole eggs from under chickens with her brother. She also told us the daring story of her cousin, Nurjahan nani, who married the cousin of her choice against her family's will. Within a generation, the marriage age shifted considerably, my mother getting married after finishing her master's. When I was growing up, the prevailing cultural norm still favored arranged marriages, but it took only a decade or two to make room for "love marriages," as we whispered admiringly about the brazen act.

My nana and nani had more than fifty years of a happy married life. Their romance was legendary in family circles. I have even read a couple of my nana's passionate letters to my nani, affectionately calling her "Monirani," my queen Moni, as her pet name was Munia. They celebrated their wedding anniversary every year. How could such affection have turned blind for fear of perceived obligation? The last few years of her life, she remained distant and disinterested, constantly worrying if she had missed a prayer. I regret avoiding going to College Street when she needed me and getting annoyed when I had to help her with namaz, but most of all I regret not being concerned about her and not trying to persuade my nana to stop the whole production of meaningless mimes by a vulnerable person. They died eleven months apart, my nana quickly after a sudden heart attack, my nani lingering on in pain, in a coma during the last few months of her life.

The four years at my nanabari, between the ages of twelve and sixteen, were a time of great confusion for me. I was passing through an awkward phase, but in the crowded house where both my grandparents' health problems loomed large, my mom became less accessible to me. My nani's advice on male-female relationships, sex, and marriage only heightened my befuddlement, my mom telling me quietly not to take her advice to heart. Chhotu was the only one who brought excitement to our lives. He was quite a celebrity by then as the wicketkeeper of the national cricket team. He made time for me and my sister in his busy life, taking us to have ice-cream cones when the first shop of that kind opened on Dhanmondi Road Number 5. Once after my sister got her cone and was contentedly walking away, she collided with someone and dropped her cone. I still remember her horrified expression. Chhotu got her a second one without batting an eyelid. I think those cones cost five taka, which was not cheap for us. In those days, the VCR had just made it to Dhaka and only very few rich people had them. Chhotu took us to his friend's place to show us E.T., which was my first movie on the VCR.

The welcome interruption in the dull routine of our lives was the stream of relatives who came without prior notice and often enough. There were some visitors whose company cheered us, like my nana's childhood friend, Mohob'da mamun nana. His name was Mahbub something, but my nani called him Mahbub'da, which sounded like Mohob'da to her young son, who failed to realize it wasn't a name and started calling him Mohob'da mamun (Mohob'da uncle), a tradition all my uncles and my mom followed. It sounded like a name to me and my cousins as well, and we started calling him Mohob'da mamun nana. He was the first committed atheist I ever knew. He challenged my nana with great humor, and my nana knew better than to engage with him. It seemed to me that he was winning all the time and without intending to he sowed doubt in my mind. He was always full of life, taking care to ask about and joke with every person, including the servants at home. I can see his tall figure striding in with a cane, full of laughter, and turning everything cheerful with his presence. As a lifelong bachelor who railed against marriage and heaven he only believed in humanity and doing good to others. There were some others too, like my mom's Mona mamu, Babu chacha, and Nurjahan nani, who were interested in us as individuals, but most of the other guests invoked routine questions about studies or irritating queries about what we liked more, English television serials versus Bangla natok, math versus literature, even abba versus amma. Too often the only consolation for wasting our time and being submerged in boredom was our share of the snacks, which were reserved for guests but could not be denied to us in front of them.

My mom's boro chacha, an avid nationalist, also left a mark on me. He celebrated every cultural event like 21 February, Pohela Boishakh, and Independence Day with such vigor and righteousness that it felt like something noble. His place at Kaltabazar buzzed with excitement, and his two daughters, three sons, and scores of nieces and nephews livened proceedings—all of them dressed in colorful sarees or pajama/panjabi—amid an abundance of food, music, and laughter. To top it off there would be cultural functions where all the attendees were performers, and songs, recitals, and even short plays were spontaneously performed. I remember writing an essay on 21 February and reading it to a roomful of people when I was fourteen. Now I suspect that a lot of people hung around as each of these events was a holiday providing a pleasant way to eat, chat, and pass the time. But Kaltabazar nana, as we called him, was dead serious. He took to heart every syllable of every poem and song glamorizing Bengali culture and nationalism. He too was an atheist, but comfortably and harmoniously coexisted with the rest of his family and extended family, who ranged from mildly religious to strictly religious. It didn't feel odd when my nana and nani, along with a few other spectators, disappeared for fifteen or twenty minutes inside the house to say their prayers, or if the performance was good, requested a namaz pause so as not to miss out on anything. The other happy memories associated with him and his household are of the yearly picnics at Betka, a little far from Dhaka, where he had cold storage facilities to store potatoes. We rented a launch and from Sadarghat, the river terminal, off we went to the semi-village, ate, ran, had fun, and returned with a bagful of potatoes, satiated from a rare day of activities.

We also visited my mother's part of the family in old Dhaka quite often, making me aware of the ambience of the old city which was so distinct from where we lived. The expeditions to Bangsal, Kaltabazar, and Shatrowza, the congested roads, the overflowing shops, and the narrow mazes of buildings belonged to another world. Often cars and rickshaws would have to stop, directly facing each other, as there was no space to maneuver; a bunch of people would appear from nowhere and guide the drivers to utilize every inch of space to make way. The traffic policeman stood in the circular elevated lonely spot surrounded by all kinds of vehicles imaginable, with his whistle largely ignored. In any case, traffic police was visible only on main roads, rarely in narrow alleys.

As much as I was reluctant to go and visit relatives in old Dhaka, which often involved a whole day with no one in my age group to play with, and paid little attention to the myriad of relatives who repeated the same familiar questions, I couldn't help being enchanted by the houses where they lived. The houses were tall narrow structures which could only grow vertically while violating all sorts of housing codes. It was astounding how many families fit into each of the narrow buildings. As sons got married, they walled off various portions of the main house to create separate enclaves, leaving unexpected walls and staircases to form tangles in the once unified house. Finding my way in the Shatrowja house was a challenge. There were four families and we had to spend equal time in all four of the separate abodes, even though there was only a flimsy wall dividing them. We also had to eat in all four places to make sure that no one would feel slighted. The Kaltabazar house, where my mom's uncle lived, had been extended with a modern adjacent unit. They lived in the merged apartment, half belonging to a bygone era, made up of solid bricks, dark, cold, and small, and the other half rectangular, sunny, and without any mystery. It was fun to cross the small bridge between the two worlds, a bridge that actually existed to connect the two parts of the house.

When I was younger, nana had a small black Volkswagen Beetle in which we piled up to visit relatives and which inevitably broke down in alleys, causing traffic to halt. My uncles would get out and push the car, along with enthusiastic onlookers who either voluntarily or being promised money helped along, my uncles swearing never to take out the car again. That car survived until the mid-eighties, even after catching fire. I dreaded those trips, as I had to sit on the lap of my grandmother who had the privilege of sitting in the front, with the rest of the group mashed in the back. My uncles and grandfather fought over who would drive, as the only other person to sit comfortably was the driver. Maybe the car broke down for good reasons!

We passed all the well-known restaurants my male friends talked about in Shakhari Bazar, a colorful section of old Dhaka, but never stopped anywhere except at sweetshops to buy sweets for whomever we were visiting. With its raucous tones and strident disposition, old Dhaka stands apart for its humor, authentic food, colorful people, and glimpses of the past. If the historic town of Charleston, South Carolina in the American South were unkempt and allowed to deteriorate and grow exponentially with millions more inhabiting the buildings, streets, roofs, and every inch of available space, it would look very much like old Dhaka.

My only hours of freedom during the drab regular days were the time in school with friends, and I stretched it out as much as I could. Nabanita started the tradition of spending the day together. Their Shegun Bagicha home was a labyrinth of twists and turns and sudden sunken passages, and the old architecture mesmerized me. The most alluring thing about Nabanita's house was her father's collection of books. I have yet to see such a comprehensive collection encompassing all genres of literature. He allowed us to read, though not to borrow, because he had sound judgment about protecting his books. Nabanita, however, often smuggled out the books, and, greedily sitting on the back bench (one had to go to school early to secure the coveted spots where one could chatter unnoticed), Suparna and I read the books in some of the classes where the teachers were lenient or unsuspecting.

I yearned to spend time at Nabanita, Suparna, and Moniza's places, all of whom had their own rooms, a luxury I had never had. Going to Nabanita's place on Green Road, where they moved when we were in class ten, took half an hour in a rickshaw; the roads were barely crowded in the eighties compared to the consistent nightmare of traffic jams today. Suparna's house was even farther away in Mohammadpur, and required a loss of two precious hours to go there and come back. Moniza's house in Azimpur was much nearer, until they moved to Mirpur, beyond the reach of rickshaws. At her Azimpur house, in front of the regular wooden door there was a collapsible gate, a transparent steel door which expanded and was kept locked. Often the key was missing, and we stood outside and chatted with Moniza who was inside and desperately looking for the key to let us in. My mom allowed me to take a rickshaw to their places, but it depended on complicated bargaining, cashing in on good grades, or her mood on particular days. My mom's permission would often be conditional: she would drop me off, if someone would bring me back. Many a times I made false promises, knowing well that all I needed was to make an arrangement to go somewhere. If I couldn't get a ride, I would surely not be left at my friend's place!

When we were in class ten and the board exam was impending, the realization that school would be over in a few weeks and the old stable ties of friendship would be tested by new connections led to a fresh commitment to spend as much time together as possible. A number of my classmates, around ten to twelve of them, walked back all the way home from school to extend our time in our last days together. The distance between Udayan Bidyalaya and our house was less than two miles, but it took almost an hour to negotiate the traffic and crowded pavements. It was winter, November or early December, the time between the pre-test and the test which qualified one to take the board exam. School ended around four p.m., after which we formed a large group and started walking. If we had any leftover money, we got some jhalmuri (a mixture of puffed rice, tomato, chili, cilantro, and mustard oil, served in a paper cone made of old newspapers) on our way out. Someone always had the money, though it was never enough for everyone. Sometimes one person's share of jhalmuri was only a fistful. Tired but determined, we started the long walk.

The wide (or so it seemed then) shaded road led to the vice chancellor's house, as we turned to the left and took the pavement because too many cars and rickshaws were going back and forth to the university on the right, crossed to the other side of the pavement to avoid the crowded University Laboratory School and Mohsin Hall and A. F. Rahman Hall, continued on the still shaded pavement to pass the University Club and other university quarter neighborhoods, and moved on toward the police checkpoint. Depending on the political situation, sometimes the bored police officers warily glanced our way, while at other times the wired barricade was pushed to the side with no visible police. The university campus ended abruptly when there were no more large trees to offer shade and solace. The small stores on both sides of Nilkhet were a jumble of tire, bedding, medicine, and photocopy stores, and suddenly one encountered a huge influx of pedestrians as well as cars, buses, and of course, rickshaws. One could see New Market as well, but this section of the road was the hardest to traverse with a thin informal pavement where hawkers set up temporary shop. When we reached New Market, friends who lived near Azimpur branched off. After an elaborate session of goodbyes (though we would be seeing each other the next day), we turned right toward Dhanmondi. The pavement surrounding New Market was more formal and elevated, but we had to pass through throngs of people who would not make room for a large group of youngsters in school uniform walking side by side. On the other side of the road, Balaka Cinema Hall was still crowded, though the three p.m. show had already started. We walked only in pairs or threesomes at the most. The boys became protective of the girls against the crowd. We started losing people left and right, at Elephant Road or the science laboratory, and I dropped out on College Street just before Dhanmondi Road Number 1. We walked like this for only a few weeks, maybe three or four or at most five weeks, but I had the most intimate discussions with my classmates during these strolls. I learned minute details of the lives of my friends, their families, their siblings, and all of their frustrations and dreams, topics I never thought of inside the school building.

The Dhaka streets never lacked hawkers of any kind. We resented sharing the walking space, but when the police occasionally attempted to clear the streets we missed the convenience of having every possible service from the cobbler to electronics sellers easily within our grasp. We were confronted with salesmen ranging from young kids to very old men, selling everything from household items to live chickens—salesmen who would not take no for an answer. There were beggars as well, again ranging in age from very young to very old. All around us, poverty was visible, all its tentacles exposed—here a small boy working at a tea stall or a disabled beggar, there a blind woman singing or a small girl selling flowers. If anything, exposure to such extremes of poverty made us immune to it. Even when we were handing out money, real empathy was hard to sustain because there were too many instances of helplessness around.

The long walks and the rickshaw rides with friends formed my relationship with Dhaka: the sounds, the smells, the heat, the sudden rain, the continuous giggles, all jostle together in recollection of the days to which I can never return. One piercing memory of a rickshaw ride still bugs me. On that day, coming back from school with Shefali, a classmate of mine who lived nearby, we both noticed a boy on a motorcycle with his friends, brazenly driving too near us, close enough to touch us. They smiled and complimented us on our beauty, which we pretended to ignore. We were bursting with anticipation, fear, and curiosity. All of a sudden, the boy threw a letter toward our rickshaw. Pretending to be insulted, I tried to catch it without being obvious, but our rickshaw turned to the right at that very moment and my first-ever love letter disappeared in the crowded road, impossible to retrieve. What was in that letter, I never ceased to wonder.

Children playing in the university quarters

The writer with her friends at Issa Khan Road

Shuvro's birthday celebration

Udayan Bidyalaya

Annual Sports Day, Udayan Bidyalaya

Rehearsal for cultural program

Mehnaaz and Papia, getting ready for cultural program

Socializing in the university quarters

Nabanita and Mehnaaz

Fun with friends at Mirpur Zoo

Identity

The Dhaka University quarters! My oasis of freedom! I can't remember a happier day in my life than when we returned to the beloved university quarters at Fuller Road opposite the Issa Khan Road quarters where we had previously lived. I was in class ten and it was 1984. The university campus provided faculty and staff several of these low-rise apartments surrounding the main university along with student halls or dorms in the heart of Dhaka. The view from the windows of our house in the university quarters was of the next building with trees and gardens in between, where one often saw people walking by and excitedly squabbling. We called our friends from the balcony, much to the chagrin of parents, yelled at the buyers of old newspapers to come up, or engaged in repartee with someone who did not want to come up. At night, we turned the lights off and the balcony became part of a faraway land, lit by stars and allowing all kinds of impossible dreams. I waited until night when the sky lit up with infinite stars to go out on the balcony and feel part of the cosmos. One of the things I miss most after living in North America is a view of the night sky full of stars.

My mom heaved a sigh of relief after returning to the university quarters as she did not have to worry about our safety as much. By that time, at sixteen, I was deemed old enough to go to a number of places by myself. I almost never had to finish errands alone. I would run into hordes of friends as soon as I stepped out and someone always agreed to go with me to New Market or wherever I was going for the sake of companionship. I never went to the Boi Mela, the bookfair, by myself. Many a times I accompanied friends to their friends' places, their relatives' places to drop off something, or on journeys without any particular destination.

In the para, one did not need to do much planning for recreation. There was a fallen tree trunk in the small and only playing field between the buildings, a popular spot in the evenings. The feeling of possession over that tree trunk extended over generations from khalammas (aunts) to young children who had to wait out their turn. After the rainy season, there was grass on the sandy patches of the field to which football players, badminton players, and younger children all laid claim. At any given time, there were people sitting around or cutting through the field to reach the main road faster. The pavement felt like an extension of our compound, or uthan, the traditional common space shared by surrounding households, rather than the street outside. It had unlimited possibilities. There were vendors selling snacks, there were groups of people here and there. One suddenly heard someone from one of the groups singing or reciting a poem.

The campus was dotted with trees and empty spaces, claimed by students and youngsters sitting around and having tea and snacks, excitedly discussing books, movies, and politics, hopping from topic to topic in an unending flow of ideas often leading to serious disputes. This is what we call adda, which can take place anywhere with any number of participants, covering any topic under the sun, yet there is a rhythm to the disjointed conversation. My recollection of such addas is that they were full of energy and passion, often involving screaming at each other as we sat in the sun with hot tea from streetside stalls or child tea-sellers.

Addas in my childhood were spontaneous and organic. How I remember Noyon stopping by, or if we were sitting on the balcony someone else might see us and come up. Or more likely, if it was not exceedingly hot, we stepped down to see who else was available and kept growing in numbers until we sat in the shade or at the corner of the pavement—the "footpath" as we called it, the word somehow capturing the informality and tempo better than "pavement." Noyon, Pasha, Ratan, Laila, Papia, Miti—I am in touch with these friends since most of them ended up on the North American continent, our identities forever shaped and bound through those memories. In retrospect, I marvel at how much I learned from those gatherings, not only in terms of substance about literature, politics, and culture, but more importantly about argument, logic, and tolerance for disagreement. Teaching in Texas in a small border city, I find that my students lack such informal settings and as a consequence political issues (I teach government) often remain confined to textbooks rather than becoming integrated as part of everyday life. Now I wonder what would have been the shape of those addas if we had had cell phones, social media, and other technologies now used regularly. Cell phones were non-existent in Bangladesh in my childhood, which spanned from the mid-seventies to the early eighties. After years of waiting, we got a residential phone, but it was expensive and we were not allowed to use it as much as we wanted to. The telephone only became a center of my life when I started seeing someone in my late teens.

We celebrated every cultural event with enthusiasm: programs commemorating Language Day, Independence Day, Victory Day, and the two Eids, along with the cycle of sports filling our lives to the hilt. There were rehearsals every couple of months: first the excitement, then frustration and panic over the arrangements, and finally commitment to come up with a good performance. The programs were filled with songs, poetry recitals, and dances, and often ended with a play. The rehearsals were a lot of fun, and everyone, including non-performers like me who sometimes recited a poem but mostly helped with the arrangements, was present. The commotions—with everyone expressing their point of view, occasional outbursts by the person in charge, and unending supplies of tea along with shingara and samosa—are part of my pleasant memories. On Fuller Road, the banyan tree surrounded by the circular cement served as one of the pillars for the stage. The makeshift stage actually consisted of cheap beds—made of plywood, locally known as chouki—rickety enough that everyone sighed with relief when the function was safely over. Year after year, these programs were staged without any professional help. We wore sarees and were spruced up from head to toe. If group recitals or songs required sarees of the same kind/color/fashion, we went door to door looking for that particular kind of saree, and parents seldom had the heart to say no to us even though they knew the risk they were taking as very few sarees would be returned without the marks of excitement, a tear in the fabric or a smear that could not be washed away.

For a young girl in Dhaka, the university quarters offered unique freedom. In contrast to other small neighborhoods, the whole area was comprised of like-minded people belonging to the same socio-economic class and roaming from one end to another, with friends allowed for almost everyone. Young girls in other residential areas often had to forego this pleasure because of safety concerns. Ironically, the military dictatorship of General Ershad that took power in the eighties added more freedom to our lives. As collective punishment to the students and faculty of Dhaka University, who refused to accept the legitimacy of military rule and barred the chancellor of the university (the president of the country, that is, the military ruler) from entering, police cordoned off the campus and erected a checkpoint where everyone was stopped and asked where they were going, the visitors often not allowed to come in. The campus became quiet and serene in the evening, making it safe for everyone who was inside. The military dictator floated a political party and had a sham election and transitioned to a president, the students remaining the only voice against him. The additional punishment was loadshedding, the electricity for the campus turned off every evening through late night. Although all the neighborhoods of Dhaka suffered from loadshedding on and off, for the university campus it became a regular occurrence, especially whenever students challenged the legitimacy of military rule. We changed our routine to finish homework by late afternoon in the daylight rather than studying in the dim light of candles or hariken. In the evening, along with the maghrib azan, the evening call for prayer, the electricity went off. In summertime, which spanned almost nine months, fractured only by the monsoon rains, it became unbearably hot. We all came out and walked in groups in the mild sweet wind of the late evening under the starry sky. Leisure during study hours was unimaginable in an environment where at least one of the parents was a teacher. Everyone was so mad and disgusted at the collective punishment that they became lax with the kids. Since the parents knew that the possibility of strangers getting past the checkpoint was minuscule, the traditional safety concerns for girls evaporated. We came up with other ways of entertainment as well. We installed car battery-powered light bulbs on top of bamboo poles which hoisted badminton nets. Badminton tournaments started as competitions between different paras, the clusters of apartments walled in with individual identities such as Fuller Road or Issa Khan Road. This identity was taken no less seriously than national identity.

I slowly got to know Dhaka through my wanderings and while each step made me conscious of my inferior gender status, my male friends did their best to compensate for the hurtful norms by accompanying me and my friends to places that were out of bounds for girls. My feelings of ownership over Dhaka were born in long walks through unknown neighborhoods in the heat, dust, and rain, exploring the mysteries it held in its concrete jungle and unexpected alleys. I remember the red rays of krishnachura and palash in the summer, the soothing mauve waves of jarul in the spring, and the dusty dark leaves in the winter. On Mirpur Road just beyond the small overpass after Road Number 7, where one could see Dhanmondi Lake—one of the very few lakes preserved in the heart of urban Dhaka—there was a house on what seemed from the distance a little island. I still see that house in my dreams.

My friend from the university quarters, Noyon, who wandered the streets of Dhaka in search of good (and cheap) places to eat, noted, "The best places are never advertised, only connoisseurs get to unearth them with diligence." He claimed that he knew the ideal places for kabab, biryani, burgers, everything that was delicious and often out of our reach. I was envious of his adventures not because of where they led him, but because he could take off any time and head anywhere in the city. Western snacks—burgers, fries, and patties—had just started to make it to regular stores from their once confined status in upscale bakeries. I can still see the small black oven where the fluffy chicken patties were kept warm, and I remember how they melted in my mouth, leaving a moist and crunchy taste to savor for hours. When I was growing up, cold drinks like Coke, Pepsi, Seven-Up, or Fanta (which disappeared and was replaced by Mirinda) had not yet replaced water, they were precious items to be devoured. Later, in the mid-eighties these drinks became available in large bottles and for the first time made it to middle-class homes. When I was a child, we only had cold drinks on special occasions. Along with packaged cold drinks, lassi made from yogurt, and sugarcane juice squeezed out in a machine, were available. Now, of course, in the overwhelming presence of many packaged fruit drinks, the only rare and precious drink on the streets is clean safe water.

Ice cream was expensive and a rare treat all through my childhood; we had to beg our parents for three taka for the elite Chockbar or two taka and fifty paisa for vanilla cups, or at least one taka for the last-resort lollypops which were essentially colored frozen sugar water. In the mid-eighties, suddenly ice-cream factories cropped up everywhere, and the local Polar brand family-size ice cream became a staple in our fridge. Later we heard the rumor that ice-cream factories started with a huge donation of milk from the Soviet Union, milk affected by the Chernobyl disaster! We never knew whether it was true or not, and while people stopped using milk in their tea, the ice-cream factories flourished. The only precaution I remember was saying "Bismillah" (in the name of Allah) before giving in to the alluring new flavors of strawberry and mango ice cream.

I got to know the streets of Dhaka by going out with friends and later with a young man in a futile search for a place to sit and converse in the city. Since half of my friends resided in the university quarters, it was easy to go anywhere with them. Often we accumulated people on our way and stopped on the pavement outside the quarters to have a grand adda. Sometimes Noyon and I went somewhere for the sake of the journey itself. If rickshaw fare had not been an impediment with our limited funds, we would have spent our entire youth on the road. Now that I sit back and remember, it seems odd that my memories are full of journeys, but not so much of destinations. Anyone who measures their experience of Dhaka with stopping points, but not the streets, misses out on much. In our late teens, a few of our luckier friends had access to family cars—boys especially had extended access since they had started driving—and we could afford to target places to spend the day. The smaller expeditions started with faraway friends' houses in Gulshan, Banani, and Baridhara, and led to picnics in the zoo, near a riverbank, underneath a recently built bridge, or along some inviting spot we happened to stumble upon.

Right after our SSC exams, a large group of friends went to the zoo and the adjacent Botanical Garden to celebrate. I had lunch at a cheap roadside restaurant for the first time. I remember eating rice, daal, and goat meat, marveling at the taste. Any food that belonged to the streets rather than home tasted superior. I, along with my friends, used to find the food at home (the staple rice, lentil, vegetable, and fish diet) monotonous and would give it up for a burger or chicken patties any day. That day at Mirpur was important as Bappi and Tanveer became part, and later the center, of the inner circle of my friends. My friends went on to many more adventures on the streets of Dhaka or even outside Dhaka, but my attention by then had veered off elsewhere. I regret all the other expeditions I didn't partake in, but which I kept using as an excuse to go out with the special person in my life.

Often, my friends Laila and Papia and I went together to New Market or Moniza's place. All three of us would get in the same rickshaw, saving the second fare by paying the rickshaw puller extra money for the third passenger. The rickshaw seat accommodated two passengers, and the third was perched on the back of the seat, legs dangling uncomfortably between the two other passengers. I often ended up in that position. As uncomfortable as it was, I remember clutching the hood, sitting a little high above everyone, and feeling heroic about it. We haggled with the rickshaw pullers as did everyone else; often we had just enough to make it to some place. Most of the major roads in Dhaka are now free of rickshaws; only certain alleys and small distances can be traveled by rickshaws. When the restrictive laws were being enacted, the rickshaw pullers were unhappy as it meant a serious blow to their livelihood, but they had to fade away to make room for imported cars and more efficient scooters. I wonder how they felt about losing their right to the city, the city where they toiled everywhere from dawn to dusk, most of it now off-limits to them.

Laila, Papia, and I started strolling in and around the campus during the long summer months after our SSC as we were waiting for admission to college and had nothing to do during that period. The pleasure of lazily reading storybooks, watching unlimited television, and even having adda with friends, which seemed justified after the intense months-long preparation for the SSC, started to wane. We walked to the TSC or the Art Institute to peek at exhibitions or at students painting or making sculptures, or the new museum on the edge of Shahbag. The museum marked where the university campus ended and my territory of freedom too, because it was the point from where I could comfortably walk home. Instead of the artifacts, what I remember are the emptiness and hushed peace of the spacious rooms and corridors, perhaps because vacant space was so rare in our lives. It was a treat to walk to the Art Institute to observe the posters on the wall and to drop by to marvel at the pictures or sculptures. I held the students at the institute in high regard, not only because of their talent, but also because of their rebellious and bohemian attitude, which I aspired to but was not bold enough to emulate. More than courage, I did not have a clear picture of what I would revolt against. My relative freedom seemed a considerable privilege in comparison to the lack that most girls of my age were doomed to go through and my happiness outweighed my worries.

After Moniza moved to Mirpur, which seemed outside the city limits at the time (ten miles from where we lived), Laila, Papia, and I decided to pay her a surprise visit. We did not call her to verify the address, which she had mentioned off-hand earlier. We simply pulled together our money and rented a scooter and without telling anyone left for Mirpur. The journey seemed never-ending, lasting more than an hour. It felt like we were crossing the urban realm and going through barren landscapes. We carried with us the sense of adventure though all we were doing was visiting a friend's place a little farther away. Once we reached Mirpur, we could not find the address we thought we remembered. The exasperated scooter driver wanted to drop us off anywhere. We ended up knocking on a stranger's house and asking to use their phone. They not only obliged us but also gave us the stern advice never to walk into a stranger's home. The story ended well that day, as Moniza's dad came with his car to pick us up. The whole time we were there, Moniza was recovering from the shock. What I realize now is how little we were warned about taking precautions against strangers. Horrible incidents involving sexual crimes were not uncommon, but never discussed. The golden rule for girls was not to stay outside after sunset, as if daytime were entirely safe. I am thankful that my upbringing did not insert caution deep into my heart, which enabled me to work and walk late at night by myself in Halifax, to live in poor neighborhoods with all their negative associations in Cleveland, and to stop anywhere and ask for directions from real human beings wherever I've been.

The pressing problem other than getting permission to go out as much as I wanted to was lack of money. Following the university quarters tradition, I earned my pocket money privately tutoring younger children on the campus. Two of my friends tutored Nausheen. My first student Parvez, a cousin of a school friend Masud, was preparing to get into Barisal Cadet College. I taught him geography and history for a couple of months and got paid handsomely. I taught Esha, my friend Pasha's sister, for a while. After finishing tutoring for the day, I stayed on chatting with Pasha, and, after he left for Oberlin College in Ohio, with his mom who felt like a friend. Esha was a superb painter who did not care much for her studies. I was heartbroken by her less than exemplary results, and Pasha's mom had to console me. My other student Dina, again a younger sister of my friend Lucy, was brilliant but believed in doing everything at the last possible moment. She had high fever just before exams and while her mother poured water on her head, I read to her from her texts. To her credit, she stood first in her class even then.

Striding along the narrow paths between the buildings and circling them endlessly was a ritual almost everyone followed within the compound. Some paraded in the morning, putting on their exercise shoes, while others strolled leisurely in the evening. People stopped along the way and joined in someone else's conversation without hesitation. The heated discussions among our fathers about academic and national politics were our inspiration to lock horns with each other about every conceivable topic. We feuded in the abstract about politics as the appealing elements of socialism and capitalism captured our imaginations to an equal extent. We were exposed to both philosophies as ways of life and knew people who religiously supported one or the other. Since Bangladesh was under a military dictatorship, there were also no current politics to discuss. We eagerly awaited the fall of the military dictatorship.

Being raised in the university quarters put us at the center of political upheaval. It was on this campus where the Pakistan Army started the crackdown in 1971 and their mass murder started with students, teachers, and staff of the university along with bewildered passersby, rickshaw pullers, and slum-dwellers who had no refuge. Shaheed Minar, which stood in silent benediction for the language martyrs of 1952, was only a couple of blocks away. Just as the families of the martyred intellectuals were witnesses to the massacre of the topmost philosophers, scientists, doctors, and writers of the country—quickly killed off by the Pakistan Army starting from 14 December as they knew that defeat was imminent, and which in fact came only two days later—it felt like every building and street had similarly been witness to history. All the dorms on the campus were named after historic figures, such as Ahsanullah Hall, Mohsin Hall, A. F. Rahman Hall, Surja Sen Hall, going all the way back to the British Raj and the revolutionaries. Bengal's history has always had a disproportionate number of rebels: from Issa Khan against Emperor Akbar, and the revolutionaries against the British, who were labeled terrorists, to the home-grown militia, Mukti Bahini, who (with support from India) split up Pakistan. Many rebel kings and social and political reformers crowd our history, known for fighting superpowers, whether it was the throne of Delhi or the British Raj. Along with the fiery spirit of Titumir who confronted the mighty British from his bamboo fort, we have also had peaceful reformers like Raja Ram Mohan Roy and Haji Muhammad Mohsin, who sought philosophical alternatives to armed resistance and created bridges between culture and religion, making religion in Bengal permeable, and Bengali identity, especially Bengali Muslim identity, unstable in the face of colliding cultural, regional, and national loyalties. Just as Bangladeshi Muslims suffer from the agonizing choice of being simultaneously Bengali and Muslim by suppressing the contrasting demands, Bengalis in West Bengal are criticized for being too provincial as Bengali identity often overpowers national identity.

The history that both parts of Bengal glorify and cherish is the history of the resistance against the British. Surja Sen, Pritilota Waddedar, Khudiram—all the figures revered and made unforgettable because their names adorned our institutions, hospitals, and streets—were regarded as terrorists by the British. Subhas Chandra Bose, perhaps the most talented politician of British Bengal, formed an army and sought support from Japan and Germany to oust the British. His silence regarding fascism remains a thorn in the Bengali psyche. We grew up learning alternate versions of history, and without ever being explicitly told we knew that interpretations of history should be challenged. I had access to many different history books, as my mother was a history professor, and these books, depending on the writer, offered conflicting versions of the events leading to the 1947 partition of India and Pakistan and the aftermath of the event. I remember being confused when my mom told me that different renditions contained partial truth. I prepared an answer combining variant understandings of Bongo Bhongo, the failed attempt to divide the province of Bengal in 1905. My history teacher, Shyamoli apa, who narrated history in the form of compelling stories, praised my effort to look beyond the official line. That was in class nine. I have never completely trusted the official interpretation of anything ever since.

Perceptions of government, institutions, and law-enforcement authorities are formed through day-to-day experiences rather than their ideal images. Even at the high pitch of nationalism, the Bangladeshi people had little respect for the institutions of government and politics, since their hopes were soon crushed by the corrupt and inefficient regime of Sheikh Mujib, the founding father, who was assassinated within four years of liberation. Sheikh Mujib was perhaps one of the most popular founders of any nation, with the precious opportunity to turn the history of poverty and exploitation around, but his political aura was mired in natural and political calamities and his brutal assassination put a temporary end to the democratic experiment. For the next fifteen years Bangladesh was ruled by the military, overtly or covertly, with different military commanders initiating their own political parties to assume a civilian posture. We came of age during a time of repeated assassinations, military dictatorships, sham votes, and student-led movements against such dictators. I find that among my students, those who come from third world countries have levels of distrust in government and the police that often mirror mine. Since I teach in an area on the U.S.-Mexico border, I have many students who grew up in or were exposed to Mexico's socio-political reality. In this almost all-Hispanic student body the difference in political attitude depends on which side of the border nourished the mind of a particular student.

We also grew up in the middle of armed violence. Student politics in Bangladesh has always been a central component of national politics; because of our history of the Language Movement and the Liberation War, students were regarded as the voice of change and just demands. The overflow of arms in the aftermath of the 1971 war, coupled with the help of politicians who wanted student support at all costs, made student groups an indomitable force in Bangladeshi politics. After the assassination of Sheikh Mujib, Major General Ziaur Rahman became president and started his own political party. He too was assassinated within four years and the army chief General Hussain Muhammad Ershad followed the same script of forming a political party, holding an election, and winning the majority. Though students were absorbed within the two political parties, fighting against army rule provided a just cause to rail against for decades. Almost everyone who grew up in the university quarters or vicinity saw students with arms prowling around during the recurring crackdowns by the police. If the army got involved, the death of students and passersby became inevitable.

Winter was our season of discontent. Every year at the end of the monsoon, when the air lost its moisture and turned pleasantly cool, the streets of Dhaka filled with demonstrators chanting angry slogans in rhyme, all of the clamor starting from the university campus. Schools scurried to finish their final exams (our academic year was January to December) before the showdown, as the repercussions included endless strikes, hartals in the local lingo, the days on which every wheel stopped moving. Oh, the hartal days! One dared not take out the car as mobs might burn it down, and very few rickshaws plied around, refusing to take the risk to cover small distances. People were expected to show up at work, but the demand was lax and the challenge of walking was taken into account; as long as one showed up late and stayed a few obligatory hours, one showed lack of sympathy with political hooligans. In essence, no work got done during hartal, plunging the country into unproductive cycles. It was especially hard for blue-collar workers, rickshaw pullers, and day laborers, whose livelihoods froze during political turmoil, no one caring about how they sustained themselves. Hartals have become more rational nowadays, as rickshaws are allowed to operate and greater leniency is shown to those performing essential functions as long as they appear to be supportive, which results in strike days without traffic jams and chaos, though the impact on the economy is just as brutal.

We did not have to worry about going to offices, facing angry mobs, or dealing with economic ruin. We woke up and absorbed the lazy pace, lying around, rambling toward our friends' houses, prattling on street corners when it felt safe. Instead of being fearful, we basked in the flurry of activities, especially the processions that started from campus and snaked around our compounds, which we joined for fun and screamed along with, having the sense to drop out near the triangle where the huge banyan tree divided the roads going to Palashi and the medical college. If we crossed Jagannath Hall, we were reprimanded for being out on the streets, but if we stayed within the boundary, we could make an argument to our parents that we were within the compound, when they were raving mad after someone (and there was always that someone) spotted us and reported us to our parents. Now it sounds like harmless adventure, but every year there were innocent people—students or passersby—who happened to be in the wrong place at the wrong time and got fatally wounded. The police used tear gas and brutal force to break up processions, people running to take refuge in our compound, where their pursuers dared not enter, though the tear gas sneaking in through the windows did not abide by any rules. We were prepared with wet handkerchiefs, but still ended up coughing and with red swollen eyes, wearing the signs as badges of honor. My association with guns and knives is not with crime but with people fighting for just causes. As a student at Cleveland State University, when I lived in the not so reputable part of downtown, the sound of gunshots did little to daunt me. After all, my mother, watching a student scampering toward the campus while fleeing the police, shouted at him, "You cannot come in with a gun! If you want to be inside the campus, go and leave your gun outside!" making the fuming student leave with the gun in his hand, head hanging in shame for violating the unwritten code of keeping firearms outside the residential compound.

We also heard rumors that marijuana was cheap and available throughout the campus and that people from all over Dhaka came in search of it. Though this was never verified, some small stores were always much busier than others, sparking understandable rumors. I had my first and only inhalation much later, at the end of the century, when a friend complied with my wish. The half a cigarette kept me laughing as I could feel the lag between my thoughts and my words, which was a little scary as I did not have full control but also rejuvenating as my thoughts became almost tangible, taking shape slowly, struggling and shifting before I could capture them in words.

Student protest and government backlash gave our environs a scary reputation, visitors thinking twice before taking the risk of being harassed by police or caught at gunpoint by youngsters robbing people to pay for drugs or for university fees as the years rolled on without exams or just for the heck of it. Anyone who went to the university from the eighties to the mid-nineties, as I did, lost precious time as our degree schedules kept dragging out because of hartals and political unrest. Universities closed indefinitely or sine die, and hartals lost their lazy allure and became obstacles to our dreams. When the Ershad government fell in the 1990 street revolution, we all felt we had participated as hope and expectation replaced pessimism and apathy toward the government, but this lasted only a few months until the two major political parties shed their masks of fighting for democracy. At least the 1990 election was a fair and enthusiastic one, where

I voted for the first time in the sanctity of the booth—which happened to be in my school—and I will always remember the excitement and bond I felt that day.

Was it hartal that made me more of a reader? There weren't many other entertainment options. There was only one television channel that started in the evening and ended at late night, local movies were silly crowd-pleasers that failed to attract educated spectators, and foreign movies were scarce and often inaccessible—and this was the era before video games and the internet. Books were scarce and expensive when I was growing up. A library card often offered only the privilege to sit and read in the library, not to borrow and bring the book home. The Dhaka University library operated on that principle, allowing students to request photocopies of several chapters at a time. The whole process took so long (though it was pretty cheap) that often one lost interest or, worse, did not need the book anymore. The public library, which had a greater variety of non-academic books, followed the same principle. As far as I remember, a lot more youngsters treated the venue as a meeting place than a scholarly destination. I only got new books for my birthday or on special occasions. The smell of a new book intoxicated me. I remember going to bed with a stack of new books after my birthday, waking up in the middle of the night and smelling them in ecstasy. The other source of funding was Eidi, the money we got from elders on Eid, which I kept aside for books and later for cassettes. My forlorn browsing melted the heart of a bookstore owner. Faisal bhai of Zeenat Book Supply not only gave me discounts, but also allowed me to borrow books. He let me do so on condition that I would buy one book for every five books I read. I happily fulfilled my part of the deal. A lot of expensive books, especially foreign ones, remained out of grasp because of the cost. I remember opting to walk to New Market, the shopping area closest to where I lived and the only one I was allowed to visit by myself, saving the two taka rickshaw fare and adding it to my fund of book money. The other treasure trove for affordable books was the second-hand market in Nilkhet, which I discovered in my mid-teens. The excitement of rummaging through piles of books in the stale air of dark crowded alleys remains a sweet memory.

Walking on the narrow elevated pavement by the stores, stopping at kiosks on the side to look at cards and stationery, I used to dream of marrying a bookseller, not having to work, and reading all day long. Fate has a quirky sense of humor. A lot of publishers send my writer husband an unending supply of books and I have been able to negotiate a few corners in our house to keep them free from piles of books. As for uninterrupted reading time, this is one blessing I am most grateful for. Going to New Market meant more than buying or looking at books. It gave me the opportunity to lay claim on my city, beyond my safe university quarters abode, a claim that few girls enjoyed. Students squatted on the pavement or the road (cars and rickshaws were not allowed within New Market) and had long addas, which youngsters looked at longingly. I had a fantasy that one day I would meet my perfect match at some bookstore. Every time I went to New Market, I felt I had grown up a little.

New Market, a mile from the university campus, was the most accessible and largest center for bookstores. There were a couple of bookstores at the stadium, which was far away, but they had greater supplies of foreign books, both English and Indian

Bengali ones. Although I loved the other bookstores on Baily Road and in Shahbag, which sprang up later, my connection with New Market stores ran deeper. As soon as I entered New Market, I turned left toward the books, cards, and stationery section. If my mom were with me, she wanted to turn right toward the more down-to-earth section with household stuff. A tug of war ensued and the winning party ended up with more time to browse in the section they preferred. The left was less crowded, and unless one was spending hours in a bookstore, the general atmosphere wasn't intrusive; we were allowed to retrieve anything from the shelves to take a good look. The bookstores were not immune to the local custom of haggling, even though the price was preset. Still it was possible to get some concessions, and now I realize how difficult it must have been for salespeople to bargain with teenagers who dug pennies from their pockets, trying to find enough to meet the price.

The exposure to English books and Western movies culminated for us at the British Council. The British Council library and theater were right on the university campus, sharing a common wall with one of the neighborhoods. The clean driveway, the colorful well-groomed garden, and the air-conditioning were things to savor. Now that I think of it, until I started working, the British Council was the only air-conditioned place I had been to. When it became too hot in the summer months, I took my homework to the British Council library and worked in the cool silent atmosphere. Unlike other libraries, we could borrow books and bring them home with a card. The card cost taka fifteen to twenty for a year, quite reasonable enough. Instead of a librarian locating the book and handing it to us from the shelves to which we had no access, we could browse through any books to find what we wanted. I remember our pathetic attempts to try to find "adult" books, then failing the courage to ask to borrow them. Often there were so many of us from the two neighborhoods that we started chattering and were thrown out of the library after a few warnings. We laid low and were respectful after such incidents, but only for a week or two. The library staff, though we irritated them incessantly, were helpful and solicitous toward young readers. The cozy little theater at the back of the library regularly showed foreign movies. Tickets for such movies were sent to members and those who had close connections with the British Council. Even though my dad got tickets once in a while, most of the movies were deemed too mature for me, and if my mom and dad missed the movie (my dad considered watching movies a punishment) they gave away the tickets to someone else. But I managed to watch a large number of movies, many of them age-inappropriate, in that theater. We waited outside the theater and begged the guard to let us in. If the theater was full, which was the case if they were showing a current or popular movie, we promised to stand in the rear of the theater and slip out before the lights came back on. The importuning went on for a long time. I don't know what made the guard give in, how much of it was kindness and how much of it exasperation. The lax atmosphere at the British Council, and the laid-back attitude toward child-rearing in general, allowed us a sneak peek into the adult world through books and movies, making it seem more exciting than it really was. The funny part about the British Council was that the guards were terribly strict with anyone who tried to steal flowers.

Shusham started a group, a sort of book club, to read books on the history and culture of Bengal. We were only in our mid-teens while the books were quite scholarly, and I felt my excitement plunging as I was handed the first bulky history book to pore over, but we did discuss it at length. This group pathchokro—study circle—didn't last long. With or without the pathchokro, Miti, Shusham, Adityo, Proteek, and I continued our discussions and analyses at home, on the streets, or when we ran into each other while getting something from the nearby shops. A more formal environment prevailed in the Bishwo Shahitto Kendro, the cultural center established by Dr. Abdullah Abu Sayeed, a renowned cultural figure who used to be my mom's colleague. The library of Bishwo Shahitto Kendro was the first one I saw with an entirely literary collection. I enrolled in a study group with Dr. Sayeed himself joining in our discussion. The first book we talked about was *Taras Bulba*, and I remember not only the plot but the detailed critique as well. The other members of the study circle were my contemporaries who engaged in fiery disputations in and out of the center. I stopped going there after a while because I started seeing someone, and as I had to cover up our meetings I used everywhere I was supposed to be going—friends' places, New Market, Bishwo Shahitto Kendro—as excuses to go out with him. I remember pining to be with my friends but unable to do so as I prioritized being with my boyfriend over all other activities.

We never had the money to buy everything we wanted, but were fortunate to be able to keep exchanging books among friends in para and school, and later at the university. Very few friends were interested in poetry, although poetry books were cheaper. Often the poetry book had wonderful illustrations, and sometimes it was a joint publication between the poet and the artist. The paper was also more carefully chosen. I remember my bookshelf with its designated poetry shelf. Through all my journeys across the oceans there are a few I have always kept with me. When I open *Haikubana* by Purnendu Potri, the magical poet of romanticism, and encounter again this artist of simple lines who contributed so much to the experiment with haiku in Bengali, I am transported to late afternoons when a seventeen-year-old waited with a throbbing heart for her new beau to return from a study tour in India, armed with letters she had written but could not send (in the pre-email days), and was mesmerized by his gift of the poetry book.

I read not only Bangla poetry, but poetry from all over the world in Bengali translation. My introduction to Baudelaire, Mayakovsky, Rilke, Nazim Hikmet, Hafiz, and Rumi, all came in Bangla. It was through poetry, trying to understand its context, that I became interested in ideas about world literature. Nirmolendu Goon single-handedly thrust me toward Russian literature and politics. Budhhodeb Bose and the dialogue among the writers of the Kollol era (Bengali modernists) about the status, direction, and future of Bangla fiction and poetry drew me toward their modernist European counterparts. The experience of Sunil Gangopadhay at the Iowa Writers Workshop was the beginning of my curiosity about the beatnik poets and the fifties and sixties in America. Years later, when I was leaving Halifax after finishing my master's, my friends gave me by Allen Ginsberg. Not only was the book as finely illustrated as Bangla poetry books, but the poems provided the warmth of a memory not shadowed by indecisions, ambiguities, and escapes.

Being in the university also meant unlimited access to nearby

Bangla Academy, the locus of cultural congregation, the site of the Boi Mela and Boishakhi Mela. Within a twenty-minute walk from home, there was a sunken dry pond and a building standing to the side like an afterthought across the green expanse of Ramna Park. The actual building was not visible from the street. The vast patch of land, more often brown and dusty than green and verdant, a large looming tree, and the dried-out pond overshadowed the unremarkable structure. February was the most educational month of the year. I yearned all year long to take lazy strolls, hang out at the bookstalls, and feel the excitement of getting the books I wanted. Now I realize how formative those experiences were. Not only was the essential habit of reading being instilled, but learning to be part of a community experience, managing the wonders and ills of a crowd where unpleasant occurrences were not uncommon, and being able to assert rightful custody of public space, were also quintessential parts of growing up. The courses I teach in urban studies have made me aware of the significance of public spaces and the shared experiences of communities of different duration. I always knew there was something special unfolding at the Boi Mela, taking place in a country with two-thirds illiterate people, that went beyond celebrating the Bangla language and the Language Movement. It was a reflection of who we wanted to be, a place and a time carved out from harsh reality, a transient dream we never gave up on.

It was at the Boi Mela one evening, under the glowing sky and amid the thinning crowd, that I discovered poetry. I remember the book, *Ontorikhe Oronno* (the forest in the sky), by Fazal Shahabuddin. It was blazing, passionate, and corporeal, making all my senses catch fire. I was transported to a new realm where each word had a smell and a rhythm all its own, clashing with the next one, producing a bewitching effect. Often the more inaccessible the poetry was, the more I was drawn to it. As if there were a magic code that I needed to break yet didn't want to fully penetrate, the journey to this half-understood world changed me. Even during the months prior to my SSC and HSC exams when storybooks were strictly prohibited, I continued reading fiction on the sly. I feel stifled if a long period passes without reading fiction. I am lucky that my profession forces me to read books, even though they are non-fiction. But the effect of poetry on me is unique. It creates new spaces, new thoughts I never knew existed. It allows me to transform the words, a line, its meaning, into my own. Reading fiction, a character or a situation takes me over, and I am transported to someone else's world, which is a delightful experience. But a poem that speaks to me becomes mine forever, to mull over and discover how it fits into my reality. During my dissertation phase, when I found Foucault, Lefebvre, and Deleuze impenetrable, I paused, read a poem, dwelt over it, and returned to the theorists, and it always worked to loosen things for me. The antidote to my nostalgia and depression has always been translating poems, which would be very handy if I translated into English as my non-Bengali husband desires, but for me translating a poem into Bengali is how I claim allegiance and go back fleetingly to my adolescence and youth.

The Bengali New Year starts in the late spring, usually mid-April, in the month of Boishakh. This is a tradition that goes back to the time of Emperor Akbar, who collected taxes after the crops were harvested from the fields in the spring, leaving the peasants to celebrate both the end of the agricultural cycle and freedom from debt after paying taxes. The Pohela Boishakh used to be an intellectual celebration of the Bengali elite in the early seventies, limited to university campuses, though now it has bloomed into a nationwide celebration. The heart of the Boishakhi celebration would start in Ramna Park, with music being played under the huge banyan tree, the botomule. The music went on from early morning until midday, with various institutions like Chhayanot taking the lead. We were up early in the morning, and wore saree—usually red and white, or some red/orange/yellow combination to commemorate spring—and were adorned with glass bangles and the spot on the forehead, the tip, and all the costume jewelry we could muster, borrowed if necessary. I remember meandering in groups, standing around to listen to music, eating the unusual snack of panta bhat—day-old rice in water with chilies, continuing the rural practice of consuming leftovers—along with the usual smattering of fruits, jhalmuri, and chotpoti, and unfortunately having to fend off the occasional groups of rowdy guys whose only interest was to create chaos and touch the girls. The unwanted touch was a painful reality of our adolescence and youth. We always had to be careful where we were going, at what time, and with whom. Our male friends were our gracious chaperones and saviors against unwelcome intrusions.

Even with the penalties women paid for the limited privilege of being present in public space, the streets, offices, and industries never lacked the presence and assertions of women. Public transport, which was notorious for unwelcome overtures, was avoided by women, unless one belonged to the lower socio-economic class and had no other options. Not only do more women work now in all sectors of life, but their visibility everywhere is more marked with each passing day. The rise of fundamentalism and the attack against women's rights represent a backlash against progress that cannot be halted or turned back. The abundance of shopping malls and other public spaces has weakened the monopoly of local goons, though these places are far from being safe from sexual misdemeanors. Public transport in Dhaka has improved a lot, in number, in discipline, and in manners. The remaining stumbling blocks are the overcrowded and bottlenecked streets which threaten to dilute all the gains made in the last few decades.

While in my generation, gender, time, and money kept part of the city off-limits to me, today it is the traffic congestion and the astounding amount of time needed to go anywhere in Dhaka, irrespective of the vehicle, that makes the city shrink for its inhabitants, men and women alike. Over the years Dhaka has grown so much that it is destined to be one of the ten megacities of the world. Growth is measured in both people and square miles, but in other significant aspects it has shrunk, allowing its inhabitants less urban space to kick back and think, to drift without purpose, to possess the city and feel connected to it.

My Dhaka never encompassed the whole city, it only extended to the areas I was familiar with and where I could go. Years later, overwhelmed at watching the first snowfall of my life in Halifax, I was walking barefoot and struck by the realization that I never had that kind of right over my own city, where I could come out of the house and walk barefoot and not worry about anything. I recited a poem by Sunil Gangopadhay which said that at midnight Kolkata is ruled by four youths ("Majhraate Kolkata shashon kore charjon jubok") and I grasped the hard truth that I had to cross oceans to be able to walk at midnight.

Love

The year was 1985. I was seventeen and he was twenty-two. He had just moved into the apartment opposite ours with his parents and sisters. Even before the obligatory visit to a new neighbor's place and the formal introductions, I could feel him looking at me from his desk on the balcony. His smiling eyes peered from behind his glasses, his hand pushed his straight black hair off his forehead, and his dark figure leaned over a model of miniature high-rises he was making for a class project—an architect in the making. I returned his gaze and started spending most of my waking hours on the balcony. His own balcony was soon converted to a cozy study with a partition, glass windows, and maroon curtains that were not drawn most of the time despite the glaring sunlight. I loved reading on the balcony, now with the added thrill, and my mother's disapproval was unable to draw me back to the safety of my own room. I could see the mop of jet-black hair over his desk, as he occasionally raised his eyes behind his glasses and his face caught up with the smile in his eyes if he caught me watching him. After a month of furtive glances, one day on my way to college he approached me, asking, "Can we meet somewhere and talk properly?" We met at a café for the first time—Mouli, the café which would become one of our favorite spots to get together. We talked for an hour, flush with fear and excitement. We did not know each other before that day, but afterwards we started seeing each other exclusively. For the next six years, that was how we would learn about each other: shifty stares across balconies, clandestine meetings, and long walks and rickshaw rides throughout Dhaka.

Dating, though it was never labeled as such, was not allowed, yet many of my friends were seeing guys. Almost every one of them had to lie to go out with someone at least during the initial period, mostly during the day, always nervous about being caught. The six years I spent trying to formulate life plans while struggling not to get caught seemed like an unwanted war imposed on me. I felt like the whole world was conspiring to stop me from seeing him. How else could I explain phones not working before half-planned events, guests coming in when I was preparing to go out, or running into relatives who pretended not to notice my companion (but later would casually mention it to my mom)?

A big chunk of my time at college (higher secondary school, equivalent to the eleventh and twelfth classes) and then university was spent not in the classroom or library, nor in addas with friends, but in trying to secure time to date. Since dating per se was not permissible, I had to steal time from studies and other leisure activities to cover it up. As long as B was a student, it worked out well as we coordinated rendezvous between our classes. BUET, or Bangladesh University of Engineering and Technology, his university, was a stone's throw from my house and a mere fifteen-minute walk from my university. Since we feared being seen by someone on campus, instead of sitting down somewhere we walked to and fro between Dhaka University and BUET through the backstreets along Jagannath Hall and Rokeya Hall, taking narrow makeshift sandy paths under the trees where the chances of being noticed by adults were minimal. Our meetings became more cumbersome when he started working, his schedule allowing him time only in the late evenings, the very time I had to be inside the house.

We spent the most amount of time sitting on opposite balconies, where we saw each other and made signs to convey messages like "Call me," "I love you," or "Let's meet outside," all our waking hours except when we were at school. We wrote to each other and dropped off notes in the mailbox in the stairwell that was rarely used, as the mailman always came to the door. In those pre-internet days, we composed handwritten letters to each other, and he made lovely cards with sketches and paintings for me. I timed my visits to either Laila or Papia's place, his next-door neighbors, when he was leaving, to steal a few moments of privacy in the staircase. These moments were reckless, as anyone might be coming up or going down and to be caught together would be an unforgivable faux pas. Every move we made to see each other was tinged with danger: meeting him near the British Council while looking out every second for familiar faces who might report back to my parents; or calling him from my parents' bedroom (which had the only phone in the house) when no one was around and pretending to talk to a friend when anyone stepped in. Each of these daring episodes bound us together and we basked in the glory of semi-revolution, as if were fighting a crusade. B and I would never have met if we hadn't happened to live on the same campus, as our interests in life diverged significantly. The excitement of having a boyfriend, being in a forbidden relationship, and fighting against all odds swept away our differences, as with ample encouragement from friends I stepped into a life of deceit and lying. My parents would never have given me permission to date someone at seventeen, though with time they looked the other way while I went on seeing a guy they did not approve of.

A stolen half an hour walking back and forth between the British Council and S. M. Hall, a planned rendezvous at Mouli when I was supposed to be out on an errand, a ride in a rickshaw to nowhere but only to be with each other, a rare couple of hours robbed from weekends—all of this culminated in romantic trysts where we risked holding hands and even quick kisses. In the six years we dated we saw only a handful of movies together. Movies in Bangladesh were of poor quality and movie theaters crowded to suffocation. All the usual hand-holding and exchanges of sweet nothings were challenges as so few sites in Dhaka were hospitable to a romantic couple. Since our plans were disrupted every moment with parental inquiries and political unrest, we put faith in chance encounters. My friend Moniza was going out with Shantonu, another BUET student, and Moniza and I took a detour through the BUET campus on our way back from college for months to see if we might run across either of our boyfriends by chance, which we never did. We never told our boyfriends of our optimistic diversion, but waited and waited for either of them to show up.

We didn't refer to a lover or a boyfriend in so many words, which was our way of insinuating the significance of the relationship without naming it. All my friends yearned to find love, but the whole universe conspired against it. We were in a big hurry because it seemed that life was passing us by without a boyfriend. Unless one was talented with musical, painting, or dancing skills, there were few choices for entertainment besides television. A cousin, a neighbor, a private tutor, the first guy we met outside the family circle, ended up being the boyfriend. Bunking off class to meet our admirers was the easiest route to romance. In college, where we had to wear uniform and could not leave until two p.m. once we entered, we carried colorful dupattas to cover our uniforms and pretend that we were outsiders or students living in residential halls to go out when we pleased. Throughout my college years I spent more time outside than inside the campus, sometimes to date, sometimes to go to New Market with friends. Between classes, we gulped down shingara at the Badrunnessa College canteen while trying not to look up at the cobwebs hanging from the dirty ceiling fan. The chotpoti-seller could barely keep up with the demands from the cluster of girls, and the common room buzzed with students catching up with assignments. This was my only two-year period of study at an all-girls institution, and we made up for the lack of male classmates by meeting our sweethearts at regular intervals.

Dating in Bangladesh, even then, was not as uncommon as people liked to believe, but it was done in secrecy and had no name. Unlike the socially sanctioned practice of meeting, eating out, and enjoying recreation that exists now, dating in Dhaka for me and my friends was marked by blatant lies or half-truths, parents suspecting but not asking too many questions for fear of knowing the reality; taking precautions about not being seen by anyone; and most irritatingly, confronting a scarcity of places to convene. Unless your family home was outside Dhaka and you lived in a dorm (the "halls" as we called them), every time you tried to step out you were confronted with questions like, "Where are you going?" "With whom?" "Who else will be there?" "When are you coming back?" or "Why do you need to be outside for such a long time?" This was the norm, although easygoing and stern parents existed on either end of the spectrum.

More than the questions and restrictions, what I resented most was the lack of privacy. Parents, maids, visitors, anyone could walk into my room anytime they wanted. I had my secret drawer, but there was no guarantee that it wouldn't be raided by my mother. I was equally guilty as I read my sister's diary to discover whom she had a crush on and felt mortified to discover that she was calling the brother of one of my friends. I had to hide every letter, every card, and every gift that B gave me, and when my friends came to visit I had to lock the door to show them off in our momentary privacy. When B made a creative desk calendar for me with small shelves to keep knickknacks, I dared to hang it over my table. My sister teased me, "Now where did you get this from?" in front of my parents, forcing me to lie, and my mother, who of course had guessed, grudgingly admitted, "Yes, it is nice, very creative!" This was the moment that bestowed semi-legitimacy upon our relationship; my mother's only remaining concern was that no relatives should know that I was going out with a guy rather than the act itself.

The most privacy we got was when we rode a rickshaw during the rain. We put the hood up for protection, and seized the plastic cover to shield ourselves. In an instant life felt worth living. The journey in a rickshaw for half an hour to an hour often offered the most private moments for couples. At the time, someone else toiling at the wheel while we sat back and relaxed did not feel like an entitlement. We enjoyed the summer breeze, the sudden rain, and the leisurely pace when we were riding in a rickshaw. Friends who had access to cars represented the epitome of freedom. Right after the rain stopped and the weak sun sparkled and the lush wet trees sparkled, I used to take the cover off the rickshaw, push back the hood, and breathe the air, fresh and heavy with the aroma of mud and trees, a smell that is impossible to capture in words—all of this now belongs to a bygone world.

If going outside the home was a struggle, finding secluded spots for trysts amounted to an adventure. Dhaka University— our nearest location, where I started classes soon after meeting B—was the perfect place for meeting and going steady, with its flexible schedule without back-to-back classes and long gaps from early morning to late afternoon; open spaces where one always found people congregating in clusters; and unending supplies of staircases, some wide and claimed by people sitting and talking, some narrow and hidden and perfectly private. University students boasted that they could tell by the body language who were the real students and who came to campus just for courting. For me it turned out to be a dangerous place. Having grown up on campus, most of the faculty members knew me, and my dad went back and forth between his office and home several times a day. Once on the street just outside Rokeya Hall, my boyfriend and I ran into my dad. My dad talked to me while ignoring the presence of the young man (quite known to him) who was uncomfortably standing to the side. It would have led to a huge drama, resulting in the cancellation of my privileges, had my mom come face to face with my boyfriend and me, but my dad chose to turn a blind eye to the situation.

Another popular spot for huddles or chilling out with friends was the TSC (Teacher-Student Center) with its beautiful open building and courtyard and its relaxed atmosphere. Students laid claim to the whole space ranging from the Administration and Arts buildings to the grassless field between the two, reaching over to the TSC, up to the boundaries of Rokeya Hall and Shamsunnahar Hall (the two women's halls at the time), and extending all the way to the Art Institute on the left, past the library. On any given day, until it turned dark, bunches of youngsters, students or not, assembled in packs, eating from the local vendors, laughing, singing, drawing, reciting poetry, and wrangling over politics. The roads surrounding the university campus were wide, with trees on both sides. In the summer, the red, orange, and yellow blooms of krishnachura, radhachura, and palash provided cover over our heads, and in the spring the light purple jarul replaced the angry energy with its serene presence. The streets were crowded with cars and rickshaws, but a good part of the road, along with the narrow pavement, bustled with pedestrians. Privacy for two young people, simultaneously nervous and brave, emerged out of the flow of strangers—a broken wall where one could perch, a clear patch in a corner littered with leaves and fallen flowers, the edge of a pavement less crowded than the rest.

The university campus was not free from petty crimes, with hijacking topping the list. Someone either walking or taking a rickshaw might be stopped and held at gunpoint or knifepoint, and everything on one's person—money, watch, jewelry—had to be handed over. The rumor was that these were university students collecting money for drug use. The police were incapable of stopping such crimes or similar ones all over Dhaka. One evening, when daylight was fading away, we were near the university library in a sequestered spot. Suddenly, there appeared a young man who first started sermonizing us over our immoral behavior, targeting me with, "Why are you out with someone who is not your husband? Do you think he will marry you?" and then threatening B, "I'll teach you a lesson for hanging out with girls." He claimed to have a knife though he never took it out. My scared offer of money was met with the vicious rebuttal, "Do you think I care for your money?" which was enough to halt my beating heart. My boyfriend handled the situation well. They started bickering but ended up parting with a handshake after a long discussion about the sanctity of our relationship. We were lucky he only wanted to act as the moral police.

Our first kiss was on the lush premises of the museum, an impressive modernist building with a cool and hushed ambiance. We went there one hot afternoon with so few people around that the comfort of crowds was not there, making us conscious of our own voices because of the echoes in the large rooms. The stern eyes of the guard followed us everywhere and soon he asked us to leave. We tried hanging out at Ramna Park, where there was ample space to relax on the concrete benches or under the shade or near the small bushes. The trouble was that the few public spaces like it had to be shared with all sorts of transgressors, prostitutes, goons, hawkers, tea sellers, nut sellers, and the like. It was impossible not to be disturbed for even five minutes by one of the small kids trying to push a sale. To make matters worse, people stopped walking to stare at couples to express their displeasure or blatant curiosity, and in extreme cases hooligans threatened with the intention of extorting money. The trick was to find a safe time when it was neither deserted nor crowded. Our quest to locate such a spot mostly ended in futility, though the memories of what felt like agony at the time are not all unpleasant now.

As my companion was a student of architecture, the beautiful Art Institute became our most hallowed grounds. Flanked by the university library and the museum, and overlooking Ramna Park, the Art Institute was probably the most creative, beautiful, welcoming, and laid-back space in Dhaka, students working on their paintings and sculptures all over the building and across the length of the sprawling garden under huge trees. Public entry to the institute was restricted except when an exhibition was going on. The exhibitions were held often and were free—a pleasant refuge from the sun, the crowds, and the peering eyes on the streets. So was Shilpakola Academy, located on the edge of the other end of Ramna Park. Along with cultural programs, painting and sculpture exhibitions were regular occurrences, and I have fond memories of walking slowly in hushed silence to absorb the colors and shapes and meanings of paintings and sculptures, feeling invigorated yet unable to articulate the reasons why some of them appealed to me while others didn't. Not knowing the grammar of art, I have always felt handicapped to explain why certain pieces of art can be so moving. I also remember the cafeteria, which was spotlessly clean. Alliance Française was the other institute regularly showcasing local and international artists. These events and spaces were the only non-hostile settings for being together with a beau, because even if we ran into people they tended to be friends and added pleasure to the rarefied evenings.

Another place in Dhaka with which I have romantic associations and fond memories is Shangshad Bhaban, our parliament building. Designed by Louis I. Kahn as one of the largest legislative buildings in the world, it was completed in the early eighties after a hiatus of ten years because of interruptions by the Liberation War and various military takeovers. The city solemnly stood aside to make space for it on the edge of busy Mirpur Road where it intersected with Bijoy Shoroni. At the time, Bijoy Shoroni, built exclusively to access Shangshad Bhaban, was the widest road in the city and to us it felt as wide as a road could ever be. During political protests this road was closed and taken over by political groups and their supporters because of its capacity to contain hundreds of people. Now the divider has marred the grandiosity of Bijoy Shoroni. We either took a scooter there or rode on B's borrowed motorcycle. The familiar Mirpur Road became busier and busier until it reached Asad Gate. After the harrowing bus terminals and narrowed street space, suddenly green space surrounded by trees appeared, with Shangshad Bhaban regally at its center. The crowds of hawkers, passersby, and visitors were unable to detract from the serene beauty of the surrounding red pavement, the sunken stairs, and the trees that guarded the building from all sides. Regardless of the vehicle one used—rickshaw, scooter, or car—one had to humbly walk a long distance to approach the main building, the only exception being parliamentarians or staff members. The walk, even on hot summer afternoons, was always under the shade. I could tilt my head a little to view the sky through young red krishnachuras, or look down at the pavement sprinkled with the fallen red flowers. Winter was especially misty because of the trees, and we had to traverse a certain distance until suddenly the enormous gray structure with its round openings would emerge from nowhere. The structure was surrounded by water, and the best spots to have intimate moments were often by the narrow waterways, a rarity in the city except in the immediate vicinity of the river. I walked along the crimson pavement and sat near the water many times. When the adjacent chandrima uddyan or moonlit garden acquired notoriety for hijackings and crimes, often a ride just to go to Shangshad Bhaban and come back slowly in a rickshaw—a ride that took two hours—would be the gist of my encounter.

When we had time, our dating voyage expanded to the Botanical Garden in Mirpur, the historic buildings of old Dhaka, and boat rides on the river to find a nook for ourselves. The Botanical Garden was vast, with enclaves made for couples to steal occasional kisses. Except for the small boys pestering us to sell peanuts, cha, or water, it was tranquil and peaceful. It was only the distance to Mirpur that kept us away from the Botanical Garden. The adjacent zoo, in contrast, depressed me. The animals did not seem well cared for and the smell was too strong, yet children gleefully rode a sickly horse or an aging elephant. The Balda Garden in old Dhaka was also delightful. It didn't open up like the Botanical Garden into vastness, but it did offer cozy and lovely green surroundings peppered with flashes of color. The Lalbagh Fort, by the Buriganga River, was a towering red brick structure, surrounded by green gardens in the middle of narrow, congested old Dhaka. The omnipresent cool breeze from the adjoining Buriganga took one back to the past—the past of opulence and pride—even if the nearby noisy, crowded, and dirty streets remained a constant reminder of the sordid present. Ahsan Manzil, another historic building, radiated a similar atmosphere; it must be much improved now that it has been preserved and turned into a museum.

We talked about our dreams: his, becoming a great architect, and leaving his signature all over the city; mine, hazy, unsure, and colored by his aspirations. He won the Mimar architecture award in a contest, which solidified his dream of becoming a famous builder one day. Never a reader, he listened attentively to what I was reading, as I shyly shared my attempts at poetry with him. He was close to his nephew, Oyon, a toddler growing up in their household, and tolerated his antics, as his sister was going through a difficult marriage and then divorce. My biggest tribulation, on the other hand, consisted of roadblocks to dating. Within a few years, my sister would be off to America to study, leaving me a room to myself. I was forever arranging and rearranging the room, concerned with finishing my studies, which were taking too long because of closures due to political clashes. When the university was closed, I had all the time in the world, whereas he had none to spare. I was competing with his demanding schedule first as an architecture student, then with the architecture firm, Sthapotik, he and his three close friends started.

Our romantic expeditions flourished against all odds for three years but came to a screeching halt the minute B finished his architecture degree and started working. The plans for Sthapotik had germinated during his student days when he, Babla, Bonu, and Rafiq Azam worked for other firms on the side. They launched Sthapotik within a year and excitedly hunted for projects and worked day and night. The only time B could spare was late evenings, when I was under much scrutiny if I were allowed to remain outside. To top it all, their family moved away from the university campus, first to faraway Savar, then thankfully to nearby Kathalbagan, still making our meetings quite untenable. I had to implore my mother to let me go downstairs to walk in the late evenings, and, although she relented, if there were too many people walking or a guest came, that was the end of my semi-date. Our encounters consisted of strolling in the compound, politely ignoring people we ran into. We sat on a fallen tree trunk when it was finally empty at dark. The most vicious hitch was neither my parents nor prying neighbors (who in retrospect weren't that prying, though we made them into enemy figures), but the mosquitoes!

We tried to perambulate around our neighborhood, but after the day's work he wanted to sit somewhere and relax a little. There were enough places for that—the fallen tree trunk within our compound, the pavements outside, especially the one by the British Council—but the mosquitoes wouldn't leave us in peace. I still remember the unpleasant sessions when we were both inclined to be romantic while the huge mosquitoes attacked us vehemently. If we had enough time, I rode with him on his motorcycle to a nearby tea stall, though the choices were limited at night. More often than not, we had less than an hour, and figuring out where to sit took away much of the precious time. My deadline to return home was nine p.m. I wouldn't have lost my glass slippers, but I never dared to bet on the rare privilege my mom had relented to and my dad was oblivious about. The whole time I was waging this battle against the world I failed to notice important differences between him and me: differences in perceptions of freedom, family, who we were, and what we wanted from each other, differences that would become crucial in my married life. The external struggle took away all the attention from the internal disparity that glared at me; it felt like together we were fighting everyone, my parents being the main impediment to living happily ever after.

Now that I think of it, perhaps it was the mosquitoes that drove us to marriage! Spending time with each other was becoming elusive and we had to fight so much for a measly couple of hours a week that we decided to resolve the problem once and for all by getting married. B was already working for his own architectural firm and I had taken my final exam to finish my undergraduate degree in the midst of political turmoil. Marriage seemed to be the only avenue to continue being together with each other. My father suggested getting admission to a master's program in India and I was interested too, but torn about the prospect of leaving my lover for an adventure of my own I chose the safer option of staying. B and I decided we would both try for admission in America after a few years, when his firm was established. Our plans and dreams were rooted in the immediate present, plotting the next meeting and how to overcome my parents' disapproval of him. My parents eventually succumbed to my wishes and started getting ready for the colorful ceremonies where they and the groom's family would play the lead role, the bride and the groom, especially the bride, relegated to the role of backdrop to the events. The preparations for the wedding, and my sister and uncle's visits for the occasion, drowned out any misgivings my parents had.

As I try to remember how the decision for the wedding came about, I am struck by the different reasons everyone preferred. For me and my boyfriend, this seemed like the ending we had always hoped for. Although our fights had started revealing sharper differences, we attributed the quarrels to external factors, mainly having too little time together. We were happy that my parents had agreed readily after being adamant against us for years. His family had always made me feel welcome, so that part was never an issue. My parents, I think, simply caved in. We never had a formal engagement—B's father came over to talk to my parents, and his mother put a ring on my finger during one of the wedding ceremonies. In 1992, my honors final year (following the British system, we used to have a three-year undergraduate degree plan), we got married with traditional ceremonies lasting several days.

We had a few celebrations, including the two gaye holuds and a joint reception for the wedding. My father detested the enormous waste typically incurred in weddings so we minimized it as much as possible. The main event of the wedding took place at a rented hall, because our home did not have space for a couple of hundred guests. Gaye holud—the quintessential ceremony where the bride is adorned with flowers, and friends and relatives wish her well by rubbing turmeric on her and feeding her sweets—was held in our home. The groom had his own gaye holud. Ripa'pa, my friend from university, made my jewelry with red flowers sewn by thread. My cousin Zafreen designed the background of the elevated wooden platform covered with colorful fabric. My back was against a built-in protruding cabinet, covered with my mom's green batik saree and rows of bright yellow flowers (gada phool) hanging from it. With all the furniture moved out, the room became spacious enough to hold the large number of people perched on our polished linoleum floor. The yellow and orange tiles of the linoleum went well with the overall décor. Nandita, my sister's friend, drew an alpona on our stairway. As the bride and groom had separate ceremonies, I never saw him and he never saw me during gaye holud. I prefer how a lot of people these days tend to have a joint gaye holud, allowing the bride and groom to experience their wedding celebrations together. My favorite memory remains the evening of gaye holud when my uncle and aunt, and my friends, especially Miti and Zafreen, sang for a couple of hours. It was July and the rain provided a welcome break from the hot weather. My sister and cousins ran around in their colorful sarees, shalwar kameez, and lehengas. Everything seemed perfect at that moment.

I was decked up for the main celebration in a heavy red saree which B's sister had selected, and gold jewelry from my mother and B's family, happy to be the center of attention. There is a tradition for the bride's sister and cousins to stop the groom at the gate and ask for money in return for letting them inside. The groom's car arrived before his party and he and his friends entered unaccosted and started walking toward the stage. Hurriedly, my sister and cousins blocked the front of the stage and held up the so-called "gate," while the lively haggling over the gate price went on for an hour, entertaining everyone. B's brother-in-law convinced my sister to take half the gate price in Iranian currency (he was visiting from Iran where he was working) which we later found out was worth next to nothing. B had designed some furniture for our room and got it made by the carpenters his company used. I had selected light mauve as the color scheme. Sitting in that room late at night, surrounded by relatives and well-wishers, I could not imagine that anything could go wrong.

I moved to an apartment in Kathalbagan, just a few miles from the university campus, with B and his family: his father, still teaching at the university, his ailing mother, and his divorced sister and her four-year-old son. Moving in with parents-in-law was expected and normal at the time. My new schedule added social obligations, but I had all the time I could legitimately spend with my husband. The irony of our relationship was that we had less time with each other from the moment we started living together. B had a serious accident a few weeks prior to the wedding and was forced to take time off from work. Right after the wedding, he started working with full vigor, determined to establish his firm, free at last from the pressure of stealing time to meet me. I would be back from my classes, fresh and primped, waiting in the dusk for my husband to return. I would be reading on my bed, my mother-in-law calling, "What are you doing? Maybe you should serve tea now," or taking a phone call from my mother or a friend or chatting with my father-in-law about the university or politics, or on the roof with my sister-in-law, waiting all the while for B to come home. All my life, I had walked outside in the evenings or at least sat on my balcony, but the apartment in Kathalbagan was surrounded by crowded streets, and the narrow strip of balcony, where a maze formed with the wet clothes hanging to dry, had barely any light and only the cacophony of the street below carried up. A sudden darkness engulfed the apartment even before sunset and my pastime of sitting on the balcony or walking outside to feel the rhythm of the afternoon slowly giving way to dusk became a thing of the past. B showed up late in the evening, exhausted from work at his firm; I wanted to go out if there was a flicker of daylight when he returned, much to the displeasure of his mom, who said, "He is tired, how can you ask him to go out? He needs rest. When will we get to see him if you go out now?" Even if we went out, we had to come back by nine p.m., to give his mom her insulin injection. She did not like the pharmacists with whom we had arranged to give her the insulin shot once in a while to allow us to stay out a few more hours. Often, he brought work home;

after dinner, I slept while he continued slogging. Our sweet stolen moments of passion and shared dreams for the future gave way to a different rhythm of life where he was tangible yet absent, and I had so much to do yet found so little pleasure.

Looking back, I now realize that we were both naïve about the expectations of marriage and our roles toward each other. B's business was taking off and he was learning to deal with the real-life challenges of his young enterprise. His alluring world of pathbreaking design was consumed by practical financial matters, which he detested but had to master quickly. Unlike me, he knew exactly who he was and what he wanted. My worries centered around finishing up my master's degree, finding a job, and ultimately going abroad for higher studies. He had been an observer of my world of politics and literature, but now I lost his attention. Never a reader himself, he had been interested in my reading list, but now our conversations lost edge as mundane problems took over. I was all for dressing up and spending time with my husband, time that he did not have for me. I began to yearn for our courting odyssey, the pilfered moments marked by inconveniences, because at least those had been my moments. Unlike our courtship days, our social life filled up with other people—visits to my mom's house, visits to other friends and relatives, and so on.

"I think it's an honor to change your name after getting married. I can't believe you're not changing your name!" B said with all the displeasure he could muster, and I retorted, "I told you before we got married that I would never change my name!" Never the one to show his anger he gave me the silent treatment, while I had to probe for days to figure out what went wrong. My need for hashing out everything and analyzing it openly was distasteful and a waste of time for him. He wanted his family, especially his mother, and me to be happy with each other. While no serious fights between me and my in-laws erupted, the differences in how we approached household chores, how we treated servants, or what constituted entertainment loomed large and began to leave dark shadows, especially for B, who told me off, "Why aren't you happy? What more do you want? I work so hard!" I had little response to B's allegations, feeling restless and unfulfilled. While B faced challenging and time-consuming demands at his company, I had to meet expectations like being present at mealtimes, managing the household staff, and providing company to my mother-in-law; soon these occupations entirely filled up my days.

The rhythm of our married life, typical for Bangladesh, was set by the workload and the everlasting presence of people at all hours. I wanted to spend a quiet day with B on our first anniversary but was surprised to find a slew of friends and relatives invited to dinner to celebrate our anniversary. I embarked on culinary experiments, but these soon became solitary chores as the hired maids avoided our house because my mother-in-law was always telling them what to do. The long-term maid Majeda had an affair with the married guard, and, after repeated quarrels with the guard's wife and eventually an abortion, left us in a quandary where we had numerous maids staying with us for a few months while I had to fill the void in the intervening weeks. If B arrived home early to help me with the chores, his mother got upset, telling him, "You're tired, get some rest," as B was the pampered only son amid three daughters. The first time I had to cook chicken for a guest, B's uncle, I was staring flabbergasted at the whole chicken, until the guest himself wandered into the kitchen and seeing the unprepared cook showed me how to slice a chicken and what parts to throw out. I fondly remember his empathy for me.

Our honeymoon, a year after our wedding, was with a tour group to India, Nepal, and Bhutan. I loved seeing Darjeeling, Kathmandu, and Sikkim. The other members of the group were single and young, quite pleasant, but I would have liked to experience the places differently than rushing around to the tourist spots. I remember so little of those ten days except for the harrowing bus rides, especially when we climbed the mountains with their hairpin curves and breathtaking scenery. That trip did little to rekindle our romance, and I remember B missing his family, which turned me off. Instead, I remember a day trip to Comilla as one of my more cherished memories after our marriage. We had gone to see a friend of mine, Ripa, or Ripa'pa as I called her, who was training at BARD (Bangladesh Academy for Rural Development), which represents an impressive ideology and institution. Founded by Akhtar Hameed Khan, the legendary development activist, it is a laboratory for experiments in self-reliance. It is set in a vast area with low-profile structures playing second fiddle to carefully maintained trees and gardens. The trip was three hours by bus. We went in the morning, spent a couple of hours, and came back the same day. I remember that occasion as distinct from our regular life. As in our courtship period, I met him in his office and we took a bus, one of the few days in our marital life when we were by ourselves. We both felt free, a feeling that kept eluding both of us as time went by.

Most surprisingly, the element in marriage which we thought was finally attainable did little to keep the spark alive. This was the part we were both waiting for: sex. Gone was the need for elaborate preparations to find a safe venue, when either of our houses was empty, which was rare indeed, or a friend's place, which involved a different set of risk factors. Premarital sex at the time in Bangladesh was taboo, not in terms of whether it took place, but in terms of no one ever acknowledging that it took place and no one ever talking about it. My own experiences and the secrets I was privy to from my closest friends' lives were contrary to the value of "sex as unpardonable sin before marriage" that every one of us was taught. Many more did not believe in it but had to remain chaste anyway because of lack of opportunities. The build-up of expectations about sex was artificially inflated with romance, because it was devoid of actual knowledge about sexuality. The accepted context of sexual knowledge was limited to safe sex and prevention methods.

Our sources of information were some horrible sex texts, a medical textbook that Moniza had stolen from her cousin, and a few friends who were studying medicine. But it wasn't as much the lack of knowledge as the lack of time and flexibility that let us down in my married life. The fact that we had to be careful to maintain our privacy through the thin walls, and the fact that other than late at night anyone could knock on the door and come in even if it was closed, only replaced the pre-marriage hurdles with a new series of difficulties. We did not know how to deal with these problems, even with each other. Later, when the logistics of our conjugal life improved, we were unable to get out of a pattern that had already been set for us by others, and, truthfully, to a large extent by us as well. Sex was relegated to late nights, once the risk of being interrupted subsided in the sleeping household, when we were both tired and angry. Going through routine motions was easier than exploring each other, connecting to each other physically and emotionally. We both believed in progressive transformation in politics, social issues, architecture, teaching, and other aspects of life, but failed miserably to take charge of our own existence and define it on our terms.

We fought against social norms to get more time with each other before we were married, but when we succeeded we saw less of each other. Our disagreements started to take up a large chunk of precious time. We could not even fight to our heart's content and express our anger and frustration as we had to whisper in rage for fear of waking up the rest of the household late at night, often the only time we would have together. Sometimes, we had to keep the water running in the shared adjacent bathroom to prevent the sounds of feuding (or occasionally the noises of pleasure) from reaching the people in the other rooms. In our wooing days, when we had an hour or at best a couple of hours a week, neither of us wanted to waste any time squabbling. We had big fights even then, always making up, knowing that the issue had not been settled. Both of us, like hordes of naïve friends and parents, thought that everything would resolve with marriage.

My father-in-law was a committed socialist bending toward the Chinese way. He welcomed political debate, but he had this invisible wall between theory and practice, allowing me absolute freedom for my theoretical points of view yet constraining me with cultural obligations in real life. For instance, nobody stopped me from going to my parents' house, but it was made clear that I was going there too much. As long as I had classes at the university, this did not emerge as an issue because I could conveniently visit my parents between classes, but later when I was working and could not manage time other than on weekends, informing my mother-in-law that I was off visiting my parents every weekend became a stressful chore. None of these issues was unusual in Bangladesh. I was the one who was unequipped to deal with such skirmishes. Neither my grandmother nor my mother had had to deal with a mother-in-law, so I missed out on exposure to negotiations in such situations. All my uncles and aunts from my parental side, except for one, at that point were living or had lived mostly outside Dhaka, eliminating the potential for family feuds. My grandfather lived in his village home, rarely coming to Dhaka and never interfering in anything. The uncles from my mom's side were in the U.S. and in Chittagong, except for my youngest one whose marriage led to similar tussles with my grandmother, often more dramatic, but soon gave way to my grandmother's deteriorating health concerns. I had missed out on a significant part of cultural training: how to handle conflicts with in-laws. More than the issues, what made the situation untenable was never hashing them out and negotiating around them.

The second year of our marriage was the first time I did not go to the Boi Mela even for a day. I asked B to make time for the Boi Mela, which he promised, but work got in the way. All of my husband's time was for his struggling firm, the dream of establishing a successful venture, creating beautiful structures in our haphazard cityscape. I admired the vision, but it swallowed up the space I needed for myself and my own dreams. By that time, I had finished my master's and started working as a research officer, first at BIDS (Bangladesh Institute of Development Studies) for a few months, and then at ICDDR,B (International Center for

Diarrheal Disease Research, Bangladesh). I excitedly waited to share the adventures of my new career, especially the field visits, only to find B tired, engrossed in his work, or drifting away to the chatter of family members. The couple of hours of television along with the rest of the family evolved as the only entertainment, diversions I shunned by quietly reading in my room much to the displeasure of the rest of the family. I went shopping with my sisters-in-law, visited relatives with my parents-in-law, and enjoyed B's company at social gatherings, but the reason we got married, to be with each other, happened less and less, and it was not as pleasant as we fought constantly. Dissatisfaction hung around like a cloud, his silence adding to the gloom, my anger unable to penetrate the unhappiness that set in with its tentacles of distance and indifference.

"Mamima, can you tell a story?" Shucheta wandered into my room and set herself up in my bed and demanded as soon as I was back from work. This three-year-old niece of B's started living with us as her parents worked outside Dhaka and kept long hours and had no childcare options. Taking care of her and spending time with her was the most uncomplicated part of my marriage. I remember the early morning tussle of getting her up and making her ready for school in her blue-and-white uniform, after which she got in a small makeshift van from her school. I made up stories which she believed to be true, and we went to Zara's birthday— my friend Nabanita's daughter who was of the same age—and Zara had a few play dates at our place. It was illuminating to study the mind of a little girl up close. Her happiness, her sadness, missing her parents, manipulating me to buy a toy, it was all so transparent. I don't know whether she remembers the evenings when she came and lay on my bed and narrated the story of her day at school, the holidays when I told her stories in the long afternoons, or the nights when she felt insecure and slept with us. It was in Canada that I most acutely missed the company of this little girl to whom I had promised a doll. Life is full of unkept promises, but this is one I wish I had kept.

The only friend I remained in touch with was Nabanita, who, as a medical student with a toddler, was herself undergoing a difficult marriage. Nabanita's star power came across in her twinkling eyes, curly hair, and alluring smile. So many boys had once wanted to be with her so eagerly, and she was unable to cope with the fact that her carefully arranged marriage was failing. She fought the wrong fight with all her energy, and after her divorce she had barely any of her feisty spirit left for herself or her brave daughter. Zara, her daughter, started supporting herself and her ailing mom when she was a teenager, and now she is on the cusp of finishing her studies and has started her own firm, the first-ever job placement firm in the country. Nabanita gave in at last to her frail kidneys and died, broken-hearted, a recluse from a life that offered so much she turned her face away from. One mistake in life, one wrong marriage, and the price exacted from a woman in Bangladesh, regardless of social stature, can be astronomical.

"Do you have field visits again?" my mother-in-law would ask, B's face would lose color in the impending crisis of my departure without a maid to take care of cooking, and I would answer, "I'll prepare food for a few days before I leave," fuming at the injustice of the workload and the lack of acknowledgement of my own career. B's cousins invited me for lunch, forgetting that I worked, and when reminded, responded nonchalantly, "Don't go to the office that day." By that time, after a year of marriage, we had moved to Uttara, a suburb of Dhaka, in an apartment that was more spacious and satisfying than the congested one in the heart of Dhaka. But the sunshine and fresh air, and the logistical upgrade to a room with our own adjacent bathroom, did little to mend our tattered marriage. B never bothered to arrange alternate options for my mother-in-law's insulin shot, so now our deadline to reach home contracted even more as Uttara was far from central Dhaka.

I can see the room in the Uttara apartment where we had to be careful to close the windows overlooking nearby construction sites to fend off the dust storm, as well as the mauve furniture, my cute red metal mirror and the small table that functioned as a dressing table, the makeshift table B made for my computer, the bamboo and jute stool bought from the Boishakhi Mela, his narrow table and chair, the bookshelf-cum-closet that was designed by him, and the stout iron almirah for our clothes. Our promises to dedicate time to each other had to wrestle with the long commute after we moved to Uttara. Although the logistics of habitation improved, our clashes worsened. Often fights were the only way to extract time and fulfill the need for being with each other. We never cleared up any issues and it felt like we were having one long-drawn-out fight with periodic breaks. Our marriage entered a more serious phase when we stopped fighting altogether.

I heaved a sigh of relief during my fieldwork in the villages, caught up with reading and able to enjoy the tranquility. I was learning about a different side of Bangladesh, but I had no one with whom to share the experiences of my career. Uttara was distant from where my friends and parents lived, so except for weekends my connection to the world was limited to the telephone. My work required long hours and a long commute, thankfully in a bus provided by my employer. Going anywhere from Uttara was expensive, unless I took a crowded public bus, where the safest place to sit (if any place was available) was in a row opposite the driver, where hot fumes burned the eyes but which was preferable to men trying to grab you in the bus packed like sardines. Any time I spent outside home—in the office, in the fields, even in the bus—became my island of solace where I did not have to deal with reality.

B had asked me to delay my plans for higher studies the previous two years, and I had relented, agreeing to wait for him, but he decided that he was needed all the more in his outfit and opted out of trying to go abroad. He left his master's program midway to devote more time to the company. The expectation for me was to continue higher studies, my PhD, in Dhaka. I, however, decided to apply to master's programs at American and Canadian universities. I started studying for the GRE on the bus during the half hours I had going to and coming back from my office. At the office, I had some colleagues who were preparing for the GRE as well. Sometimes, I stayed back and worked on math problems to take advantage of uninterrupted time to study. My cousin Samina, twenty days younger than me, had a kid a couple of weeks before I left. My husband and I went to see the boy who was born a little early and we both realized that we had missed out on this experience. Three years of marriage was considered too long for a couple to remain childless.

I remember the night I finally decided to take my destiny in my own hands. It was a windy, rainy evening, and I was returning to Uttara in the late evening, which was not deemed safe, especially for a young woman. The scooter kept sputtering and stalling every fifteen to twenty minutes, and I held my breath as I recalled stories of hijackers and scooter drivers planning crimes together and expected to see someone jump into the scooter at any moment. Although I dreaded it, part of me anticipated the calamity with glee, knowing how sorry my loved ones, especially my husband, would feel if they lost me. The scooter driver talked constantly, which I took to be a sign of his guilt. He didn't look too nice either. As it turned out, he was only a talkative person with a bad engine. He dropped me off at the marketplace at Uttara Sector 7 and said that his scooter wouldn't be able to make the remaining distance to Sector 10, a distance of five more minutes. Since it was raining hard by then, I decided to take shelter at the marketplace before taking a rickshaw home. The street hawker was shielding his books from the rain and bundling them up and offering discounts as he had to rush off because of the inclement weather. I bent and picked up Barron's guide to the GRE, the cheaper version published in India, the print so small I had to squint at the yellowish pages which could not be any thinner. I remember the black cover with red, yellow, and green stripes which felt as heavy as my heart. The seller was offering a thirty taka reduction, taka one hundred and seventy instead of two hundred. I had the money on me and on a whim I bought it and probably sealed my fate and the fate of my marriage in that split-second decision.

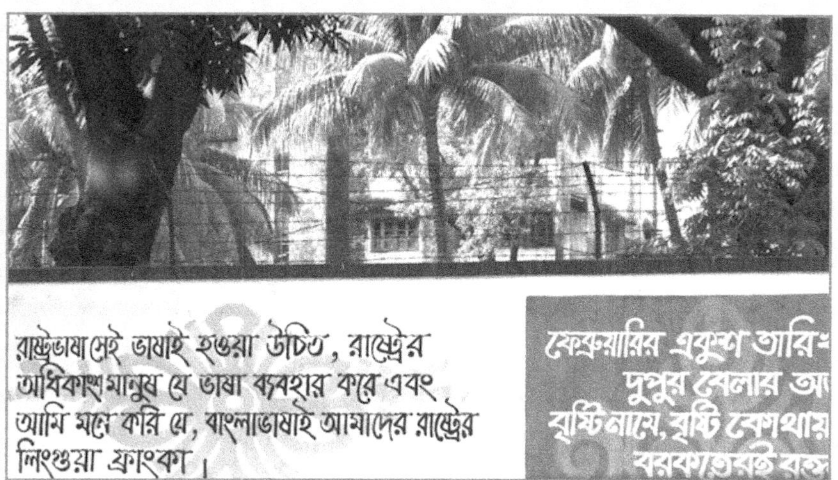

Ekushe February

Dhaka University quarters

Love

Dhaka University quarters

Students at Dhaka University

Rickshaw ride in the rain

Art Institute

Curzon Hall

The bench at Fuller Road quarters

Public Administration students at Oporajeyo Bangla

Cox's Bazar study tour

Waiting

If I had to summarize my university experience in one word, it would be waiting. After finishing the HSC we had to wait for months to take our qualifying exam, which kept being postponed for no apparent reason (even my father, a faculty member at Dhaka University, was unable to get the inside scoop on the elusive date of the exam). After the exam there was a heart-wrenching wait for another couple of months for the result and the interview that determined our major, and after that we had to wait again until the university had enough classroom space and faculty to teach us. Meanwhile, several cohorts were stuck in the same academic year because of the sharp political divisions and the consequent prolonged closure of the universities. These session jams, like traffic jams, stalled our life, only in more magnified form. We were forced to spend six to seven years to finish three years' worth of a degree as our university remained closed for more than half the year. Every time there were any political demonstrations or rallies by students, the government closed the university indefinitely and waited a couple of months for the turmoil to die down before reopening the university. Year after year, these unplanned closures accumulated in lost time, and students had to remain much longer than the allotted year of their coursework simply to take exams. It took me seven years to finish my three-year BSS and one-year MSS. My final exam was cancelled and rescheduled thirteen times over an eleven-month span.

In 1987, after waiting fifteen months, we finally started our classes one fall morning. At last it was my legitimate entry to my own backyard. Dhaka University was not only a university, it was also the nation's cultural mecca and political barometer. Now my claim to its proprietorship was formalized. It was the excitement of being an adult in a world where professors deferred to us with the formal "apni" as the prerogative of an elder rather than the customary "tumi." It was the green island of freedom in the concrete jungle of Dhaka where one could roam about with friends/boyfriends/girlfriends, face off endlessly about politics, films, and books, and flirt in the safe comfort of large groups or a secluded niche for two. The class schedule allowed large intervals intended for the library but most students used the opportunity to engage with classmates.

The sculpture Oporajeyo Bangla (unvanquished Bengal), commemorating our war of independence, stood in its glory at the center of the university. The three imposing freedom fighters in white stone—the student, the farmer, and the nurse—lent the character and spirit the buildings generally lacked. Dhaka University had lost its cream of intellectuals when at the end of the war the Pakistan Army started rounding up intellectuals and murdering them. Students, especially those who resided in the halls, were killed viciously on the first day of the attack on 26 March, 1971. The campus was an appropriate location for this two-story high sculpture of three people reflecting commitment on their faces, standing tall in front of the Arts Building. It became the logical choice to start rallies. Many a times, I stood on the fourth floor, looking down at the gathering crowd, sometimes with mute support, sometimes with frustration as I foresaw another interruption in my studies.

The Arts Building was an efficient white four-story building whose sole purpose was to provide maximum classroom space. The classrooms, the corridors, every element was so uniformly designed that there was never an unexpected turn unless a particular stair had been blocked. The most non-functional and beguiling part of the building was the long balcony wrapping it on all sides, allowing the breeze to come in and providing space to relax. A corner of the fourth floor had been converted to a canteen with a girls-only sitting area (and two precious restrooms), so that the boys could not go inside the canteen to order snacks and tea. It was one of the most popular spots for the boys to hang out, as they waited for the little boy who worked in the canteen to come out and take orders, or requested fellow classmates privileged enough to walk into the girls-only area to place orders. If the intention of maintaining the all-girls common room (there was another on the first floor) was to provide a secluded niche for girls, the outcome was the opposite. The girls were not unhappy about the boys intruding on their privacy, and often gave up the option to sit under the noisy old ceiling fans and ate outside the common room to enjoy their proximity. There were no common rooms for the guys, which did not seem to bother them.

The fields in front of and to the sides of Oporajeyo Bangla were always filled with students conversing in groups, even on bristling summer days when the temperature reached the upper nineties. I remember a number of trees, kolaboti and jarul, whose shaded areas were the prime locations. The huge banyan tree which now stands atop an elevated platform was the seedling planted by Senator Ted Kennedy when he visited newly independent Bangladesh in 1972. As the only senator who dared to protest the Nixon administration policy of aiding Pakistan to continue its genocide in the eastern half, he sought to bring attention to the refugees by proclaiming the situation "one of the most appalling tides of human misery in modern times." My dad was present at the tree-planting ceremony where the senator received a jubilant reception in the independent nation.

The most popular location for adda was the Teacher-Student Center, or TSC as we called it. Designed in 1961 by Constantinos A. Doxiadis, a Greek architect-planner, it was the most beautiful building on campus. The low-rise building was open and inviting with its spacious courtyard and the large arches of its cafeteria. At its center was the huge auditorium, indispensable for cultural events, its acoustical quality suitable for large audiences. The open fields inside, the pavilion outside, even the stairs were always crowded with students. A low brick wall cut off the sheltered space from the rest of the world, the design allowing for a glimpse inside. The design also permitted the cool breeze to flow in, even on scorching days. The solitude of a pair amid the boisterous crowd, or brawls among large groups at the top of one's lungs, were equally tolerated and prevalent on these grounds.

The spots outside were no less popular, especially after a famous sculptor, Shamim Sikder, erected one of her masterpieces, Shoparjito Shadhinota (self-earned independence), on the small green triangle outside the TSC. We were students at the time when Islamic fundamentalist groups threatened to smash the sculpture made up of joyful figures celebrating independence, because human figures in public squares, according to the fundamentalists, were tantamount to idols and hence sinful. Sikder, a black belt in karate, vowed to beat anyone who would dare to harm her work. We waited on tenterhooks, but the inauguration day went by without violence. The small patch of land with the magnificent sculpture in the middle evolved as a magnet for snack sellers, and I spent many an evening relaxing on the grass, the monument close enough to me to marvel at the intricate design of the figurines, munching happily on shingara, samosa, or chotpoti.

Most of our classes were conducted in Bangla and English simultaneously, the professor repeating in English what he or she had just enunciated in Bangla. Very few professors taught entirely in Bangla. We had the option to write either in Bangla or English. At the time there were only a handful of schools, expensive private ones, which were English medium. So whoever chose to write in English, like me, was in most cases writing in English for the first time. Fifteen to twenty percent of the class selected English, while the rest chose Bangla. The blackboard and chalk were the only equipment available to the professor, who stood on a dais, resorting to hollering to reach the back of the class. There were rows of long tables and benches capable of seating as many as ten students in large classes, but usually seven or eight of us assembled comfortably. There was no taboo in sitting beside boys, because we all preferred to sit next to our friends. None of our classes had assigned textbooks. Often we did not know which textbook the professor was using. We had the syllabus and came to the lecture, but preparing for exams was our responsibility. We had to go to the library to search for books on similar topics and make our own notes. If I had to change a single component of higher education, it would be getting rid of assigned textbooks. One of my most shocking experiences as a graduate student in Canada and America was to discover that each class had an assigned text and the professor was beholden to it. As an academic I realize that it makes my work easier, but it turns the purpose of higher education on its head. Instead of analysis and judgment, we prompt students to believe in a singular viewpoint. We might add alternatives and question the assumptions behind the assigned reading, but there is no getting away from the fact that structurally the not so subtle message is that the preferred text contains all one needs to know for the course.

Looking for books in the low-rise white square library on the edge of campus was not a joke. In the pre-internet era of card catalogs, one needed the exact title or author to request a book as students did not have access to library stacks. We took the information about the book to the staff standing in the islands between the reading area and the precious shelves, which we could only gaze at from afar, and they brought the books to us. The scarcity of books and the volume of students forced an unusual practice at the Dhaka University library: students did not have borrowing privileges. We could sit in the reading area and prepare and take notes as long as we did not leave the library premises. Even multiple copies of most books were not available. One had to plan to go very early or right after lunchtime or stay until dusk when most students left to get the most sought-after books. We were not allowed to bring anything but paper and pen inside the library. There was a small cubbyhole through which we had to deposit our bags and receive tags for our stuff. During exam rush, disposing the bag and acquiring the tag could end up taking an hour. People often worked in groups. I remember studying with Nayeem and Mahbub, sometimes Sania, before the exams. The reading rooms, which were at the center of each floor, were never silent. The low rumble among animated students went on constantly, and when it reached a high pitch, the staff—I remember middle-aged men with beards or weary annoyed students—warned everyone to keep it low, and the library settled back into its rhythm of hushed waves of cacophony.

Theoretically one could request large sections of books to be photocopied, but the bureaucratic process took weeks. I knew students who held sway over the personnel and were able to get the books out for a couple of hours to make photocopies of certain chapters. I took advantage of my dad being a faculty member by forcefully sharing his privilege of getting ten books at a time for two weeks. We fought over who would get what number of books for how many days. I always thought the system was punitive to students, but now from the other side of the table I can't imagine how professors sustained their research and teaching in those conditions. The library usually did not have recent selections. Because my major was public administration, I could take advantage of a number of institutes which mainly trained government employees or management personnel and had the budget to order the latest books and journals. Starting from the Bangladesh Institute of Management in Sobhanbag, which was far from campus, to the even farther National Institute of Local Government at Agargaon, or the National Institute of Public Administration at Savar, which was outside Dhaka, I ventured out in search of books and journals. If one knew someone at these centers it helped tremendously, but in general people rewarded the enthusiastic student's request to use the library and allowed limited borrowing privileges. After investing so much time and effort, one had to study those books, if only to justify the sweat and toil spent in acquiring them.

I have few memories of actual learning except for classes with Ahmed Shafiqul Huque, Habib Zafarullah, and Salahuddin M. Aminuzzaman. The fifty-minute classroom lectures were typically impersonal. We also had tutorials with professors in small groups, ten or fifteen at most, where we had the opportunity to engage in topics at length and procure assignments that we enjoyed. At the end of the third year we had to undertake the organizational analysis of a real institution and for the first time apply our classroom learning. Aside from that exercise and the field trip to Savar for the elective course on project administration (the students who took rural development went to BARD in Comilla), no hands-on learning went on.

Although in keeping with my identity as a good student I ran back and forth from library to library, I learnt more about the reality of politics and administration in Bangladesh by engaging in lively discourse with friends, especially those with a pronounced political bent. The books and the bulk of lectures had little connection to our cultural setting. Had I not worked in Bangladesh, especially in the rural setting, my knowledge of the real Bangladesh would have remained pitiful. Among our classmates, boys were more frustrated with the gap between classroom teaching and reality. They were accustomed to dealing with real-life issues such as running errands, paying bills, dealing with telephone linemen, protesting if charges had already been paid. If one did not belong to the affluent class, the path ahead was mired with unfair competition (whom you knew mattered more than what you knew) for low-paid public sector jobs and the scantier private sector jobs. For girls the pressure to get married outweighed the pressure to land a good job.

My commitment as a lifelong good student had instilled a mental bar which did not let me play truant, although I did occasionally skip the large subsidiary classes which were similar to a minor and graded only pass/fail, creating a disincentive to do well. These classes tended to be humongous, with two to three hundred students, and took place invariably in the late afternoon, a perfect time to sneak out and have a tête-à-tête with a friend or lover in the shade. I was severely punished by fate for such actions once. There was a large political science class being held in a newly constructed lecture hall. Sitting in the back, I could barely hear anything. The doors behind kept beckoning me. I took the brave decision of taking a short leap when the professor was facing the blackboard. I had seen other students do the same, so I knew the door was unlocked. All I had to do was open the door unseen and the spiraling stairs awaited to lead me to freedom. I ran to the door and fled unseen but was not prepared for the scene that confronted me. The other aspiring students who had performed the brave deed minutes ago were standing with sour expressions on their faces, melting away in the narrow hallway. The stairs were blocked with fallen branches. We were not the only ones to have had the bright idea. The university administration had preempted us. There was no way we could climb down the stairs and we could not sneak back into the class either. In the scorching sun, we had no other option but to wait for the class to finish.

The recurring violence among students and the closure of the university soured our attitude as we started looking forward to the days when we could complete classes without unforeseen occurrences. Student politics in Bangladesh has a proud history of standing up to unjust rulers, students being in the forefront of our language movement of 1952 and the 1969 revolution leading to the Liberation War. Dhaka University students were the first victims of Pakistan's military atrocity when the army orchestrated mass murder in the university dorms in 1971. After liberation and alignment with the ruling party, students were at first put on a pedestal, only to fall from grace along with the Awami League, the political party besieged by various unethical and corrupt practices. The Mujib government and his Awami League fell from power with the assassination of Sheikh Mujib in 1975 and the takeover by the military regime of General Zia. When Zia sought to legitimize his military rule through the newly formed Bangladesh Nationalist Party, or BNP, its student arm played a pivotal role in the formation and legitimization of that party. The clashes—both verbal and physical, often involving arms, between student workers of the Awami League and the BNP—started erupting much too often on campus. Within four years, Zia was assassinated by yet another military dictator, General Ershad, which prompted an uneasy alliance between the two aggressive student bodies. Ershad floated his own political party, the Jatiyo Party, but it never gained traction on campus. The decade of the eighties on campus was the decade of infighting among the Awami League, the BNP, the Jatiyo Party, the rising Islamist Shibir, and a few other weaker leftist and progressive student groups.

The Islami Chhatro Shibir, or Shibir as it is known, accumulated its political power in the eighties. They were not only ruthless but very well-organized with a small but fiercely loyal following. A few of our classmates, both boys and girls, belonged to the cadre, persuading us to listen to their polemics without getting angry. The passion of left-leaning students groups like Chhatro Union was quite different, theoretical and somewhat theatrical in nature. By the time I started university life in the late eighties, after more than a decade of military rule people had suppressed the memory of the violent displays of student power and the presence of arms in the post-liberation period and remembered only the courage of students in leading the anti-military movement that had started to gain momentum. The abuse of student power had not yet started, and students were again back in the category of those who spoke truth to power in the face of danger.

We would be sitting in class listening to Lutful Huq sir on development administration and hear Molotov cocktails blowing up outside amid blood-curdling screams. At first we used to duck under the desks, then we gathered enough courage to look out from the window or adjacent balcony, and by the end of our degree plan we were merely irritated and our professor resumed the class after the obligatory commotion if there were no other ominous signs. It was difficult to concentrate on mundane theories of government when even faint-hearted girls who had tears in their eyes shrieked, "Oh no, not again!" within a year of the first experience. Political parties were banned during the military regime from 1980 to 1990, but their student wings made up for the missing clamor. The Awami League, the BNP, the Jatiyo Party, and the Shibir cadre fought with each other, among themselves, and with the police. These fights continued for hours, the university cordoned off by the police, students stuck inside to wait out the inevitable raid and questioning. Back in the eighties, females were rarely stopped, but our male friends, especially those who lived in the dorms, told us about the harassment they faced, ranging from blows to arrests.

I remember a class which was shelved again and again because of political clashes. Finally Akhter sir was eagerly finishing up the chapter on budgeting and it seemed like we would get to take our impending test which had already been rescheduled three or four times. As the lecture was nearing the end with only fifteen minutes left for the class to be over—the professor was explaining zero-based budgeting—a fresh surge of shooting began. I will never forget his beseeching voice, "I only need five more minutes!" as students started ducking under the desks. By that time we knew to huddle beneath the tables, closing our eyes and if possible covering them with wet handkerchiefs to avoid the fumes of tear gas. After coughing and shielding our red eyes, we had to be careful not to venture into empty streets because this signaled an impending fight. We knew we had to stay put with lots of people as the police hesitated to harass large groups and to leave the campus only when it became safe once the police strolled in after the end of the fight. The low-paid police officers were usually on the defensive, attacking only after they were attacked. The moment police presence was visible was the moment firing ceased. The police were not our protectors; rather, they were an appendage of the gutless military government, standing guard at the checkpoints surrounding the campus with their needless suspicions. To enter campus one had to answer whether one lived inside, but there was no absolute proof of this, which meant that it was up to the discretion of the police if they believed someone or not. We were not afraid to respond curtly as the police rarely harassed girls and very seldom used their weapons against students.

We became so accustomed to the sounds of firing that when the early morning raids in the dorms adjacent to our apartment in the university quarters woke us up, we cursed, "Why can't the bastards fight later on in the day?" because of lost sleep. I remember my mother being upset at gunshots in the afternoons, complaining, "Your father's lunch will get cold. Who knows when he'll be able to get out?" or "There goes my siesta!" rarely fearing for his safety. The faculty had immunity unless they happened to be in the wrong place at the wrong time. Our homes were certainly in the wrong place though. If fights occurred in the next building, Salimullah Hall, we had to close our windows to keep out the tear gas. We kept wet towels and handkerchiefs handy during disturbances.

By the late eighties I could proudly distinguish the sound of gunshots from that of petrol bombs. Not only were political activists roughed up and killed, but students or bystanders also got caught in the mayhem and died of shots not intended for them. One such stray bullet grazed my friend Noyon's hand, brushing him when he was standing outside the university quarters. As these protests intensified in the late eighties, the military slowly replaced the local police to fight off students and other civilian demonstrators. The military's high-handed response to student protests ended in a lot of dead students and common citizens, and twice, in 1989 and 1990, people took to the streets to oust the Ershad government. While the 1989 movement fizzled out—we only had three months of classes that year—in 1990 the dictator Ershad had to hand over power to an interim government. The students, indeed, had led the movement, and by being witness to it all, I felt I had participated in a revolution. The euphoria on campus after the fall of Ershad was palpable. People greeted complete strangers with great verve and spontaneous musical concerts occurred day and night.

I voted for the first time in my country in 1991. My old school, Udayan Bidyalaya, across the road from our apartment in the university quarters, overflowed with people bursting with excitement. That day, patiently standing in line felt like a patriotic duty. Little did we know that we would only get caught up between two corrupt regimes, the Awami League and the BNP, who would form the government turn by turn, and with each cycle outdo the other in inefficiency and blatant power grabs. Students now don't have to suffer through session jams though the in-fighting among student groups continues unabated. Employment opportunities in both the private and non-profit sectors have grown to phenomenal levels. Although only a small percentage of students is active in politics, they are the ones who are dominant on campus. Student politics in Bangladesh has never ceased to be associated with the political parties who hire, employ, and exploit students to keep their power alive while turning a blind eye toward the use of arms, bribery, collection of money, and displays of wanton force by their supposedly idealistic activists.

As a student and educator in the U.S., I now cherish the informal and haphazard methods of learning even if we were not encouraged to do enough critical thinking. Our acquaintances and books made up for what was not formally part of our curriculum. It seemed like we were part of a continuous colloquy with friends, conversations always branching off from one direction to another—books, movies, politics, religion, nothing was off-limits. Although we were surrounded by people all the time, there was more time for reflection as well. The homework took a couple of hours in the evening. Before we were allowed to go out to play until dusk, there were several hours in the afternoon for naps, reading, or being by ourselves. We had to create our own world mainly through books as we had few other sources of entertainment. Our television had one national channel, video games did not exist, and good movies or in fact any movies other than the weekly one on television were rare. Our inner world was sustained by the force of our own imagination. In all my years in Canada and America, what I have missed most is the precious time of dupur, or afternoon, where I felt the world stopped for me. The hot afternoons were slow, lonely, and permissive, and somehow the thoughts and acts during this period seemed to persist outside the normal flow. I lost this cherished time when I started working, but even at the office, just after the lunch hour everything slowed down and there was a gradual transition to reality. When I was a child most of my dupurbela was spent reading, lying on the cool cement on the balcony shaded by the overgrown trees, and when I grew into my teens, this was the time to talk to my lover on the phone or daring to go out to meet with him.

During my university days, when not in class, dupurbela was for long lazy addas with intimates, or stopping by at Imtiaz bhai's office for a couple of stimulating hours. Imtiaz bhai, who had had both my parents as his teachers, was himself a professor of international relations. He continually prodded me to write, advice I did not take seriously. I looked up to both Imtiaz bhai and his wife Foara apa as mentors who were accessible for any discussion imaginable. More than the large formal classes, mostly devoid of participation, I remember the occasional conversations with my professors when I stopped by with questions or the small tutorials where everyone was compelled to participate.

I remember a class where we were sweating away as the electricity was gone, when Nazmul Ahsan Kalimullah—the young professor who had just returned from Britain after his PhD, and wore T-shirts to class, much to the dismay of older professors—proposed that we step outside in the breeze to finish the class. I don't remember the content of the class, but I do recall lounging on the grass, getting surprised stares from other students, and sipping tea while hearing the lecture and asking questions. There were no computers, no internet, and no PowerPoint slides during my student years. We may have lacked the technology, but what we did have was ample downtime, not cluttered with games or entertainment or a frenzy of activities. The learning moment, which is private and intimate, often does not take place in the classroom, thus it is not necessarily captured or reproduced through cutting-edge methodology.

So much of my university days was spent congregating outside the classroom and engaging in debates, waiting for classes to resume, and plotting safe welcoming places to meet my beau, that I am amazed I managed to learn anything. Truth be told, the formal component in the classroom was inadequate as we learned mostly about Western government with very little emphasis on our own system. Flocking outside, we blew off our anger and frustration regarding learning, politics, our future. Students who aspired to join the civil service complained, "How long do I have to remain a student and ask my parents for money? Time is running out. If I can't graduate before I'm twenty-five, I won't be eligible to sit for the BCS exam. I'm from a middle-class family, I don't have connections to the elite. Without government service, no other employment opportunities exist for me." Boys taunted us, "You girls have it easy, all you have to do is get married!" while the girls retorted, "Can you imagine handling the pressures of a career and getting married at the same time?" Unemployment was high and the private sector was frail in the late eighties. Some of us had plans to go abroad for higher studies, though we did not know much about the process, and were only holding on to a distant dream.

Even though higher education was highly subsidized in Bangladesh with minimal tuition (less than a dollar per month), students who came from outside Dhaka had to bear the cost of lodging and food, which was closer to its real cost. For poor parents it was a burden to bear without knowing when their sons and daughters would graduate. No employment opportunities for students existed in the formal job market; the most that was possible was to earn pocket money by privately tutoring schoolchildren. On top of that, the Dhaka University halls or dorms were insufficient to the demand for such facilities, which was five times higher than the supply. To make it worse, the dorms were controlled by student leaders who pushed for party workers over students. A number of party workers enrolled as students, never took exams, and hung around the halls to be able to work for the student wing of their party. Student leaders often skipped exams to hold on to their positions so they could stay year after year, until the university at last amended its lax examination policies.

Although we socialized with students from other departments as well as our own, the identity of each academic department became dominant during interdepartmental sports, especially cricket. How can I describe the feverish excitement of a cricket match lasting a whole day? It is somewhat comparable to enthusiasm for football teams at American universities, but being the only game in town it meant so much more to us. Perhaps cricket is the British legacy that the Indian subcontinent has most successfully assimilated and made its own. Classes were cancelled during semi-final or final matches. More enthusiastic professors like Mohabbat Khan, Salahuddin M. Aminuzzaman, and Habib Zafarullah put in appearances and stayed long to encourage players. We walked together in large groups to the Dhaka University stadium, a twenty-minute jaunt to the vast field and its solid cement pavilion. Quite a few of my fondest memories are of sitting all day long with my class friends and cheering on the players, "Four! Six!" even when they managed to score only single runs. I don't remember our department winning a game but the mild winter rays of sun in the gallery, the continual snacks of nuts, jhalmuri, and ice cream, and the hoarse voices shouting "Out!" to demoralize the other team remain etched in my memory.

What I remember distinctly about my university days is the mode of perpetual transition, from the few idle months when the university was closed to the excited frenzy of reopening, only to give way to another bout of violence, followed by the deserted campus where we hung around to get any information about when classes would restart. My great solace in those days was fiction, as I had all the time in the world and nothing to do. I reread every book that was in our house, and borrowed books from friends in the university quarters as often as possible. I tried developing hobbies like learning how to make flowers with paper and cloth, but soon ran out of ideas for new flowers and got bored with the process of starching, cutting, and shaping the cloth pieces into flower petals and joining them with leaves made of paper and wired stems covered with paper. My motivation evaporated as I started each day with the physically draining thought, "Is there anything interesting in my life?"

At the university, Nayeem, Sania, Rupa, Rais, everyone seemed frustrated with the present. The only dream to indulge in was to go to America or Canada or Australia for higher studies so we asked around for information regarding the TOEFL and the GRE, jealously thinking of friends who had gone to the U.S. or the Soviet Union after the HSC exam and were now finished with their studies. My third-year final honors exam had been delayed eleven times over a nine-month period. Every time I felt I was well prepared, a clash between students and government would move it further away. The last time the exam was cancelled was on the very day of the exam. My cousin Zafreen, my dad, and I were walking toward the university at around a quarter to two as our exam was supposed to begin at two-thirty. My dad had just proclaimed, "You two will finally be able to take your exams," as we crossed over to the pavement adjacent to the vice-chancellor's bungalow. We could see the Arts building, the exam hall on the fourth floor accessible only through a side stairway that remained locked for the rest of the year. All we had to do was cross the street to get there. The firing started right at that moment. Instead of running away, we stood there, mute in disbelief. We were so close. My dad said, "Go home, I'll see what's going on." Totally unconcerned about his safety, we responded, "Call us if by any chance the exams are being held!" Of course, the call never came. Rather, we received commiserating visits from our class friends who could not make it to the exam hall but were already on campus when the firing started. Another group of students was trapped inside the exam hall as the shooting went on. Finally, it was either in February or March of 1992, after six years in the university, that we had our third-year final honors exam. Instead of experiencing stress, all I remember hearing is, "Oh, this is finally happening!" and feeling the same myself.

The wait for the results was also an agonizingly long process which could take a month to several months involving a complex labyrinth of bureaucracy with internal and external examiners and third examiners if there were big enough disparities between the internal and external examiners. We were spared further waste of time because the university decided to go ahead and let us start the master's coursework. All the hard work of years came down to a few days of exams. For each paper thirty percent of the grade was from in-class exams and tutorials, and the rest was the yearly exam with essay questions. If one was sick or going through problems during exam week, that pretty much determined the score. We had to take only one paper at the end of the first year, three at the end of the second year, and five at the end of the third year.

Meanwhile, girls were getting married left and right. My school friends Nabanita and Moniza were married very early, barely at twenty. Nabanita continued in medical school while Moniza moved to Boston with her husband. Among my classmates, I remember a few weddings, the most poignant being Laiju's who was supposed to join her husband in the U.S., but as our exam kept shifting, her husband gave her an ultimatum and she had to follow him, leaving her studies. A lingering fear reigned in the minds of our parents that we would be less desirable as brides when we finally completed our education and started working or if we waited around to get married. I too joined the ranks of the married in 1992 between my honors and master's program. My honors result, where I topped the class, came out the day after my wedding, making everything seem perfect.

While I remember the impatience and frustration of the first six years to get through my three-year degree plan, the last year of the master's program seemed to fly by. I was adjusting to my unfamiliar married status and was suddenly thrown out of the safe cocoon of university life into the uncertain job market. I was envious of my friends who went to medicine or engineering schools where they had a stronger bond with a smaller cohort. Dhaka University was too big and unorganized compared to the elite engineering and medical schools. Everything seemed more haphazard, from classes and exams to social and cultural events. As the cultural focus of the city, the university held many events commemorating Independence Day, Language Movement Day, the first day of the Bengali New Year, and the first day of spring, which stand out in my memory as enchanting occasions filled with music, poetry, and camaraderie. After the coursework was finally over and the results published, I would be in a rickshaw passing by the university and could not think of any good reason to stop by even if I felt a nagging tug that I had left something behind.

The most memorable part of the master's program was our study tour to Cox's Bazar. Every department arranged a study tour, usually overseas to India, Pakistan, Nepal, or Sri Lanka, ranging from several days to a couple of weeks. We heard stories of previous batches and their fun-filled excursions to India, but a boy and a girl had been caught there while they were intimate and that spelled the end of any foreign trips. After a lot of imploring, our jaunt was downgraded to a domestic one, and while some whined, some others, especially girls, were relieved as getting permission from home to go to Cox's Bazar was easier than securing consent to go to India. We had followed the traditional way to collect funds by publishing a magazine where we persuaded some companies to run advertisements. That money covered some of our costs, the department gave us some funding, and we had to make up for the rest. A greater challenge was to find a professor willing to accompany us as no one was motivated to take time off and spend money to go to nearby Cox's Bazar. At last our mellow and jovial Asad sir relented even though his wife was expecting a baby at any moment. As it turned out he had to cut his trip short to be with his wife while his youngest son was being born. Our trip would have been impossible without a professor, and being the most mild-mannered and pleasant faculty member he gave in to our unreasonable demand.

I had to wait until I was twenty-four to go on a five-day trip with my friends, chaperoned by a professor, in December 1992. There were about twenty-five to thirty people in our group, less than half the class, as a lot of the girls' parents could not imagine the horror of young people of both sexes spending time together. One of my class friends relayed her mother's shocked response, "Impossible!" I had been married for six months at the time and glowed in the good fortune of not having to seek permission from anyone. We boarded a train from Kamalapur station in the late evening and reached Chittagong (only a hundred and thirty miles away) in the morning. The train with its worn-out wooden benches could hardly contain our joy, a freedom beckoned that we had never felt, and we babbled all night long with occasional dozing. We had a few hours in Chittagong before catching the bus to Cox's Bazar and one of our classmates took us all to his home for a hearty breakfast. The local bus to Cox's Bazar, which was less than a hundred miles but a good four hours away, was not as comfortable as the train, but the excitement made up for all the discomfort.

I had visited Cox's Bazar with my family in greater luxury, but the cheap motel called Pantho Nibash, with eight beds to a room for all the girls and two larger rooms for the boys, is my happiest memory of the place. We were acutely aware that these were the last days of student life, which, with all its flaws, had protected us from the reality of the world so far. "This is it!" "Who knows whether we will be in touch or not?" "Our lives will be so different from each other's soon," we murmured to each other. Because it was a study tour, there were a couple of educational items on our agenda, but I have no memory of them. What I remember is daring to sit on the edge of the boat without knowing how to swim, the fresh salty air on my face and hair, and the smell of freedom to do anything I pleased. I remember a night in a rickshaw with my friend, Dipa, when we got separated from the others and were suddenly all by ourselves in the dark landscape. Dipa's anxious voice rang in my ears, "I hope the rickshaw puller knows the way, we certainly don't!" but as I looked up, my fears evaporated. The vast unending sky was lit up with stars, the dimmed brightness reflected on the dark dull silhouette of the sea. The feeling of being part of such beauty and yet realizing my own insignificance lingers as one of my most cherished moments.

We visited all the desirable spots as a group, and ate at the small crowded street stands where freshly caught pomfret fish was fried and served in a jiffy. Sometimes the food stands had to borrow chairs from their rivals to accommodate all of us. At the time, even though Cox's Bazar was the most popular tourist destination, it was mostly left alone save for the few hotels. The majestic Parjatan hotel, too pricey for locals unless one belonged to the elite class, pretty much stood by itself facing the shore. A few umbrellas and deckchairs belonging to the hotel huddled nearby and some foreigners graced the privileged corners. The cheaper hotels and the few rest houses to which only top-level government employees had access were far from the shoreline. The tourists were mainly local young men bathing in the water or loitering on the sand, making way for the few lucky motorcycles and jeeps cruising along on the beach, with far fewer women walking or daring to take a bath fully dressed. Swimming costumes for women are forbidden in Bangladeshi culture, even now. We disregarded the gaping stares of men by splashing water and letting the high waves take away all of our embarrassment.

We visited the waterfall in Nuliachhori, rode a boat to the nearby island of Moheshkhali, where the air smelled of dried fish, and went to the Burmese market on the edge of the Bangladesh-

Myanmar border. The Rohingya people of Burma had not yet been driven out of their homeland to seek refuge in Bangladesh. The border was porous, and as some courageous fellows strolled carelessly and entered Burma, the handful of Bangladeshi and Burmese soldiers lazily told them to go back to Bangladeshi soil. There was not even a no-man's-land between the two countries. The Naf River below served as the natural boundary line with its bright white line of foam surrounded by various shades of green. Upstream at the market, young Burmese girls, with ever-smiling faces and adorned in their marks of sandalwood, sold Burmese products: towels, sandalwood boxes, sandals, and colorful clothes. Now I know that the lazy pace of life and the playful waves of the Naf River were only an anomaly, waiting to be filled with the plight of refugees fleeing massacre, as the border would soon be closed and tightly guarded, and the boatsful of refugees on the Naf River would be turned away to their death.

I also remember the realization that I knew so little about my classmates. After the final exams, most of my classmates disappeared into oblivion and although I stayed in Dhaka for three more years, with the exception of Nayeem, Sania, and Monower, I lost touch with all of them. It is only lately, after twenty years, that I am again in touch with some of my friends courtesy of Facebook. My university days were filled with the frustrations of a long wait to finish my degree. My classes with the long breaks certainly did not prepare me for the real world. Still I remain grateful to Dhaka University, where I spent my formative years, for the confusing journey, for the luxury of long interregnums to read and reflect, for forcing me to chart my own path.

Reality

Like the Dhaka-centered economic and political topography of Bangladesh, my own existence was centered in Dhaka. The two yearly trips to Kuliarchar and an occasional trip every couple of years to Chittagong where my uncle lived were the only instances when I could see Bangladesh outside Dhaka. Even then, these trips were always inside closed circles, meeting and spending time with extended family members. I learnt about life in Bangladesh other than my own surroundings in Dhaka from the girls and women who worked as helping hands in our home. Kamala, who stayed at our place for over twelve years, before marrying and settling down with her own family, hailed from Manikganj, an area barely outside Dhaka (I am shockingly looking at the distance I just googled, a mere sixty-seven kilometers or forty-one miles). She used to beg us to write letters for her. We wrote very similar letters asking the same questions of one of her uncles every three months or so, while she waited for a reply in the meantime. If she was not going to Manikganj physically, which she did every couple of years, these letters were her only means of communication with her village and her aloof kin. Surmising from these letters, life was slow, stagnant, and dull as soon as it crossed Dhaka. Kamala now lives with her family in Narshingdi, a little farther off (ninety-six kilometers or sixty miles) and calls my mom every week from her cell phone and visits her every couple of months. The time for the journey may have only halved, but neither Manikganj or Narshingdi nor a host of other semi-urban small towns are distant from Dhaka anymore.

My first and most enduring exposure to Bangladesh outside Dhaka came through fieldwork. As a graduate student, I was involved in a project headed by one of my professors, Salahuddin M. Aminuzzaman, which took me to Mymensingh, Comilla, and Barisal. All three trips lasted for two to three days, as I hastily conducted interviews with the recipients of CARE, our client for the project. These were my first trips without at least one of my parents. I remember relishing the freedom, the new sense of responsibility as a researcher, and the anticipation and anguish when my professor asked about my interpretation of our work. That was the first time my views and indeed I as a person were taken seriously. I was acutely aware of my new authority while dealing with other NGO employees. My first night away from home was in Mymensingh. I was full of a sense of adventure and even the mundane task of filling out survey questionnaires felt heroic and purposeful. We stayed at BARD, the institution of cooperative societies that is internationally acclaimed and was established by Akhtar Hameed Khan in Comilla. I remember lying awake and listening to the rain as I tried to mull over the excitement of the day. Barisal was so green and lush that at every twist and turn we encountered water, often a river, a small tributary, or a pond that reflected the bright green which was so different from the dark dusty green I was used to at my village home. We went to very poor households which were typically the recipients of NGO services. Even indigent homes seemed clean and bright surrounded by so much greenery and water.

The project I was involved in had to do with the reorganization of CARE, an international NGO. Although we went to the program areas and talked to the recipients, the bulk of the work involved going through documentation and interviewing field employees. This was my first hands-on experience as I was still studying at the university. Salahuddin sir had selected me and Nayeem, a classmate and close friend, to work with him. We were more than foot soldiers as our perceptions, analyses, and assessments were being taken into consideration for the new organization plan. The salary we drew for those three months made us feel rich, but nothing could top the confidence that we came out with at the end of the project. Afterwards, anytime I was doing anything on my own, I realized how much I had learnt from this single exposure to real organizational issues. More strikingly, I became aware of the huge staff who worked in the field areas of remote villages and whose skills and knowledge were so much more useful than my theoretical learning. NGOs in Bangladesh created employment opportunities for a huge mass between the skilled and unskilled levels, and for women they opened up a job market that had never existed before. In a country with pressing unemployment and abundant labor, it was only the educated, particularly from excellent institutions, who were hired, leaving behind a huge batch of young people, usually from a lower socio-economic background and with degrees from smaller colleges in rural areas and townships. For women living in the villages or small cities, there was no option but to wait to get married after they finished their schooling. The people who were not exactly poor and uneducated, pressured to maintain their social status a notch above the working poor but trapped in a system that offered no avenue to white-collar jobs, remained absent from political discourse. The spillover effect of mushrooming NGOs was the creation of employment in rural areas, which allowed people to hang on to their home turf, focused on getting jobs rather than acquiring academic degrees, and to live their lives with newfound confidence and dignity. Analysis of NGOs in Bangladesh tends to concentrate on the recipients, ignoring the large group of people who fill the low-paid but exacting job of fieldwork and link the privileged world and the world of the poor with real data, information, and insights, as they have access to both worlds.

My professional exposure allowed me to witness and study the social changes that NGOs were instigating. All the theories of gender equality cannot teach men what they can learn from working with women. I was surprised by the beliefs and attitudes of a lot of fieldworkers who were more progressive than my friends at Dhaka University. I also became sharply aware of how much I did not know about my own country and the limitations of my academic training. Each field visit was educational and transitional for me. By that time, my marriage had become burdensome, filled with expectations and disappointments on both sides. Fieldwork, which often involved overnight stays in villages, provided me with much needed relief. It yielded the time and space I had been unable to create for myself at my in-laws' place.

I also became aware of my own privileges because for the first time I was comparing myself with colleagues from different backgrounds. I knew how lucky I was to have had progressive parents, to have grown up in a liberal enclave in Dhaka, and to have had the freedom of choice in making important decisions, but I had not known just how fortunate I was. It is the accident of birth that determines so many of our life choices. In Bangladesh, it established whether you went to college and which one, which in turn predicted your opportunities. So many people deserved a better education, but their family's economic situation would not allow it. I encountered many who would have excelled in academics, their social and political understanding deeply rooted in reality. A lot of primary research was built on the sweat and ideas of fieldworkers and researchers alike, but fieldworkers rarely got credit. It was natural to swap stories of juggling home and work and speculate about our future aspirations with my coworkers. I knew it would be comparatively easier for me to get over my setbacks and reach for my dreams. The fieldworkers who were married had to walk a tightrope between the demands of family and career, relegating their own dreams to the backburner.

After my master's exam, I started my first full-time position as a researcher at BIDS (Bangladesh Institute of Development Studies), and after six months I joined ICDDR,B, an international research organization where I worked for close to two years. Both of these positions offered me the opportunity to take a close look at Bangladesh, its raw neglected element, its people for whom Dhaka was as far as the moon, their beliefs, aspirations, and opportunities, or more precisely lack thereof, but mostly another rhythm of life, which had been so close yet so far from me in my early years. This was also the period when I was going through a rough time in my own life. I was flabbergasted at the discovery that after dating a person for six years and fighting with my parents to marry him, I had not reached the "happily ever after" stage and was consumed with guilt, confusion, and desperation. I treated my field trips as a break from real life, promising not to think about my own problems. I honed in on my work, the fascinating new world whose language and decorum provided unexpected surprises which I tried to decode with rigor and some misplaced passion. I began to understand more about myself when I became curious about other people's lives, and I did it because of the nature of my research but also because I was genuinely intrigued. Studying the poorest of the poor women, the recipients of NGO programs, I was shocked to discover similarities in aspirations and paradoxes, something my comparatively elite educational background had not prepared me for. When asking intrusive questions driven by research needs, I was forced to think about my own answers. I saw the real Bangladesh in those two years, and I saw a person in the mirror who looked like me yet was so different than what I had believed her to be.

The memories of my first formal job are of long rickshaw rides to BIDS in the surrounding thick mist; pulling my shawl closer and trying to squint through the mist to view the buildings in Agargaon, especially the radio station, to see how much closer I was to BIDS; and the sudden bumps followed by the descent to broken roads leading through the noisy slum toward buildings that stood indifferently. After teaching students at regular intervals and conducting irregular assignments as research assistant to various projects, at last I was hired and paid by an institution. I landed the job, a hands-on research position to replenish my empty resume until I found a career path, through word of mouth. I was familiar with the BIDS library and the library next door in the local government institute where I had scavenged for current reports and journals not available at the Dhaka University library.

But the idea of working in the neat angular building, having my own cubicle even if it only consisted of a table and chair in the middle of the office, and finding university friends such as Miti and Arif as fellow research assistants, constituted unmitigated joy.

My job involved not only the secondary research of finding facts and data, but also primary information collected through interviews and surveys. Instead of being cooped up in the library poring over dusty reports and journals, this meant rickshaw and scooter rides throughout the city, the apprehension of meeting new people, the assertion of my position, the satisfaction of getting the tasks done, the agony of bureaucratic roadblocks, and the unexpected lessons which seemed inconsequential at the time. Primary research also offered control and flexibility over my own time. I was slowly being exposed to another world where the poor were not only beggars and maidservants but had dignity, rights, and demands of their own. I remember an organization in Mirpur which provided underprivileged girls with technical know-how. I was enjoying the new knowledge and unaccustomed liberty in the company of friends. It was sheer luck that my childhood friend Miti and university friends Arif and Opu worked at BIDS at the same time as I did. Often we ended up in the library at the same time, our hushed talk and animated faces prompting the stern librarian to caution us about proper decorum for research assistants in the library. We heeded such advice only fleetingly. If we were not in the field, we had lunch together. Instead of the proper but dull canteen at BIDS, we ventured to roadside stalls—noisy and messy, with day laborers and rickshaw pullers as customers, and food that was cheap, spicy, and good. We meandered along muddy and broken roads to get to the small restaurants with bamboo roofs, asked for the rickety wooden benches to be wiped clean, and ate with full appetites in disdain of health and safety precautions. I would pay more attention to the conversation of the other customers, the laborers and rickshaw pullers, were I to visit such a place now. At the time, full of youth and energy, everything centered around us. All of us are in very different places now, but I am sure each of us cherishes the uncertainty, spontaneity, and sheer thrill of those moments.

The most memorable experience at BIDS was the two-week-long field trip to the northern part of Bangladesh. We went to Dinajpur and Rangpur, up to Kurigram, the northern tip of Bangladesh. We traveled in an SUV with Dr. Simeen Mahmud, her foreign co-researcher, a cheerful young girl who worked as her translator, her right-hand man Bashir, the driver, and myself. It was early summer and the air-conditioned car was more comfortable than the outdoors, although occasionally we felt a pleasant breeze during long stretches when we conducted interviews in village homes without electricity. As we drove endlessly through the red dust, the pressure of having conversations with superiors, that too in English so as not to alienate our foreign colleague, hung in the air. We tried to translate chitchat and realized how challenging it was. I was not comfortable with spoken English as I had never had to speak in English in any forum. Even if I was comfortable in writing, it was different to carry out an everyday conversation than to write an essay. We often exchanged jokes, which were the hardest to translate. The tone and nuance, which contain the essential meaning, and often the puns, were lost in translation. I remember our collective struggles in translation. A woman we interviewed, a silent and docile one, was a group leader, an unusual situation since group leaders have to be assertive. Upon enquiring we learnt that she had been married to someone in her ancestral village, which meant that she knew all the influential men in her village and had access to them unlike other women who came to the village through marriage. It was a smart decision by the group to elect her as leader because of her unencumbered latitude with the local elite who had known her since birth. We had a difficult time explaining the protocol of this non-kinship tie to our foreign researcher, who was trying to grasp the maze of social rituals we instinctively understood. The elation generally outweighed the exasperation of translating cultural nuances.

We were impressed by the deep tubewells dug by the World Bank, which later proved to be a vehicle for arsenic poisoning. The dry and often drought-ridden northern part of Bangladesh requires an ample supply of water for agricultural production. Tubewells provided by international organizations like the World Bank seemed like a boon. But as people dug deeper and deeper, arsenic seeped into drinking and irrigation water. It took a few decades for the impact of arsenic poisoning to manifest, while people became continually sick with new sets of related diseases. The slow response of the government did little to alleviate the pain and misfortune of the afflicted people. As there were no alternatives besides those tubewells, people had to continue to cook, clean, and irrigate with the infected water, and even drink it, knowing the harm it was causing. No international agencies were held accountable for their lack of knowledge and no politician paid any price for not protecting the public interest.

We were oblivious to the looming problem as were the host of NGOs, both domestic and international. This was more in-depth than my experience with CARE, and, more importantly, this was from the point of view of the recipients rather than the NGO itself. A number of weaknesses of NGO activities were becoming clear to me. We encountered a women's group, who got a loan to irrigate a piece of agricultural land, which they found out was too sandy for cultivation. The ever-creative women took the engine off the irrigation machine and installed it on a boat, and the money they earned from the boat was more than what they had hoped for from irrigation. It also demanded less time and labor. Instead of getting credit for their ingenuity, they were harassed and pressured by the NGO (Grameen Bank) to put the engine back on the irrigation machine where it belonged. It was a reflection of bureaucratic rigidity, because that particular women's group had been showcased as a successful female association working in the agricultural field, a rarity. The image of the NGO was deemed more important than the real impact, as questions of ownership and authority over the loan by the recipients were ignored.

The regional variations in Bangladesh were also becoming clearer to me. I realized that the women of the Mymensingh region, where my ancestral village was located, had a reputation for working shamelessly with men in the fields. The deep level of poverty explained their aptitude. The expression for "I miss you" in the Mymensingh vernacular is "pet pure," meaning "my stomach is burning," no doubt influenced by the same awareness and sensitivity to poverty. Social norms, especially when it came to gender, varied in different regions as well. Regions which at one time had a Hindu population had adopted Hindu cultural norms seamlessly. I was shocked to learn that in many instances the woman was not given the "mehr," or bride price, she was entitled to according to even the narrowest Islamic edicts, but often got back her dowry. Much to my surprise I found that adopting a girl in a household without girls was nearly as common as adopting boys. Adoption has never been esteemed in Islam, and in a country with a high birthrate and high poverty it was not a common practice in my social circles. The social stigma against adoption was more prevalent among the middle-class and the rich as the poor often practiced it for utilitarian reasons: adopting a girl meant a pair of hands helping with household chores, whereas adopting a boy meant economic security. In the last twenty years not only has the stigma evaporated, but people have also become more open and honest about adoption.

The culmination of my learning took place at ICDDR,B, my next job, where I held the position of researcher for a little over a year. It was an international health research organization with its reputable hospital complex and adjoining impressive building in busy Mohakhali in the heart of Dhaka. Beginning as a center that did research only on cholera, ICDDR,B addressed a vast array of health issues, easily expanding into social issues. I worked at a joint project between ICDDR,B and BRAC, another well-known NGO in Bangladesh, on gender issues. ICDDR,B's laboratory was in a village called Matlab, situated in Comilla, a hundred miles from Dhaka. ICDDR,B's hospital provided free medication to people in return for intensive data collection every two weeks. The data became a vehicle for various health research organizations all over the world. BRAC, on the other hand, had just started their projects at Matlab and lacked benchmark data. The intention was to utilize the rich databank to explore the health impact of the social and economic projects of NGOs. My first assignment involved primary research, interviewing divorced, widowed, and abandoned women to analyze the extent to which NGO programs had reached and helped them.

The topic of my research proved depressing, especially when I could offer no help to women who were giving me their time and trusting me with their undisclosed stories. Nevertheless, my memories of Matlab are full of jubilation. The journey to Matlab itself was enjoyable. The office microbus took us to a riverbank where we got on speedboats. It was the fastest way, taking less than three hours from the main office to the field office. It was possible to conduct research and return to Dhaka by nightfall, as our bosses did. Not only was I required to spend more time in the field, I enjoyed spending more time there. This too was a project where I was on my own. We had the option of staying at the elite guest house of ICDDR,B where five-course lunches and dinners were served and air-conditioned rooms were available, or in the guest rooms at the BRAC office where we had to share meals with local officers at their mess and split rooms with other guests. The elite aura of ICDDR,B often proved to be a hindrance in breaking ice with not only interviewees but fieldworkers as well. Soon, I discovered a better arrangement in the study villages where field researchers rented mud and tin houses, people gladly accommodating visitors from Dhaka and divulging stories invaluable for understanding rural life. The major flaw was the substandard bathroom: to take a shower, I had to stand in a place surrounded by three bamboo walls which meant that I had to take a shower fully clothed and then run back to the cottage to change. The water was red, heavy, and full of iron; just one shower and my hair turned sticky and brittle at the same time. The few times I opted to stay at the ICDDR,B guesthouse, I was lured not by food or air-conditioning, but the luxury of a private shower.

I soon learnt that developing trust and having an open attitude were more valuable to research than all the theoretical techniques I had been taught. I selected shabby clothes when interviewing and covered my head with a dupatta. This simple act had the power of signaling that I was not so different from the local people. Walking in the dusty field for hours under the blazing sun, it made sense to cover the head anyway. Islam adopted the Arab custom of head covering which was essential for both men and women in the desert before modern technology provided relief from the sun. It is amazing how functionality can get divorced from ideology, and how ideology can create its own meanings devoid of alternative opinions, while passions run wild among both supporters and opponents.

I interviewed seventeen women in-depth, four or five times each, each interview at least an hour. A disturbing pattern emerged. In each instance the woman had been hurriedly married off, the father choosing to shift the burden without adequate knowledge of where he was dislocating the burden to, and then becoming frustrated as his mission backfired once the woman, after being divorced or abandoned, often with a child or two, came back a heavier burden than before. For land-starved and heavily populated Comilla, adjacent Dhaka beckoned the unemployed, and men left for the city looking for jobs and never returned. I remember a Hindu widow whispering to us that her husband had paid a bride price to her father according to the customs of her caste. We found this custom of reverse dowry remarkable, except that in neither situation did the woman get any control over her dowry.

The fieldwork started early in the morning, soon after sunrise, so that we could finish talking to the women early enough to allow them time to cook the meal for the men in the household getting ready with their ploughs and cows. The other busy time for the women to finish household chores was late afternoon, when the husbands came back from the fields. Between late morning and early afternoon, the personalities of the women changed drastically. Gone were their careful head covers, hurried steps, and busy hands. They still did their chores, but at a more leisurely pace, talking and laughing with one another. Even though I dealt with single women, they all lived with their fathers or brothers and expected to put in more labor in return for free food and lodging.

The fieldwork involved taking long walks of many miles through narrow dusty paths full of children playing and running, crossing a single bamboo pole over a small pond, taking rickshaw rides along the uneven muddy road, and venturing on occasional boat trips on the river. I was always accompanied by local fieldworkers who knew most of the recipients of NGO projects intimately. Their insights were more valuable than my contribution, which was to apply research techniques and communication skills. More than work or research, informal conversation with them changed my outlook. I had been blessed by the accident of birth, yet there were many common concerns that we shared. The phase of fighting and rage in my marriage was over, as I was resigned and trying to define a sphere of my own. The lesson I learnt from my research subjects and coworkers was never to give up on my dreams. All the women I interviewed lived in great hardship, yet each of them had a dream and a plan for a better life.

The field visits became my break from the stifling world of routine and labor and having no time for myself. They started early in the morning but were over by mid-afternoon. Even after writing down the notes, or checking on other datasets, there was ample time on hand. A number of NGO workers were housed in the office building. Not only were there people to talk to, there was also the riverbank along which to walk alone or in a group, the crowded haat or market to observe the crescendo of rural life, and the sudden twists and turns of the winding paths, which were seasonally surrounded by sugarcane. The deep green leaves of the young bamboo trees, the hazy reflection in the not so clean water, the statuesque banyan trees, and the daring small bushes of wildflowers, all welcomed me to their world. I used to tell myself that I wouldn't worry about any problems or heartaches as the field visits were a holiday from real life. I didn't always succeed, but the visits did calm me down. Often I took a book of fiction with me, for which I could not make time in Dhaka, and the contentment would make my life seem worthwhile. Later, when I started preparing for the GRE, I would take only Barron's guide to utilize the precious undisturbed time. Sitting in the dark study village, with only the hariken illuminating a twisted oval space that barely covered the book, intense concentration on the small print of the slippery thin paper of the guide became my way out of the impasse. The BRAC office had electricity and the ICCDDR,B office had air-conditioning, but I opted mostly to stay in the study villages, optimizing my time to prepare for the GRE.

At the Dhaka office, I spent most of my time with my comrades-in-arms at work—Santosh, Munir, Jahangir, and Maria—to substitute for the gaping absence of friends. Like me they had been sucked into practical realities and were devoting all their time to shaping a career for themselves. ICDDR,B had a charming canteen, highly subsidized as well. The food was delicious and cheap. We used to go to the canteen together, along with other colleagues, and spend as much time as possible there for not only lunch but also the two tea breaks. The conversations during meals started a lot of friendships that are still alive. Because of the reputation of the food, the canteen attracted a number of outsiders, people working at offices adjacent to ICDDR,B, and occasionally the staff complained that the food was gone before they had the opportunity to eat. Then for a week or so everything would become strict and one had to wear the ICDDR,B badge to prove that one indeed worked there, but the rules tended to become lax after a short period of scrutiny. Since this was an international organization, the canteen was open during the holy month of Ramazan, when everyone was supposed to fast. I saw many people from other offices at our canteen, sometimes even friends and relatives who worked in nearby offices.

There was a television in the canteen, which was usually drowned out by the voices of people, but which became the center of attention during sports events. People were inclined to spend so much time for lunch and tea breaks during cricket matches that the director sent a memo for the television to be muted. I remember people bringing in small radios to listen to the commentary while watching the television screen during cricket matches. There was a cricket match where Bangladesh beat India for the first time in early 1995. I was working in my office when I heard the blood-curdling screams from the canteen. The few of us who remained in their offices rushed out to join the unbridled celebration.

I enjoyed my vocation, not only for personal reasons, but for the challenge, and the confidence I derived from it. I had to present my findings at internal seminars and in front of donor agencies or renowned researchers in the field, dreading the public speaking part. The lessons I learnt about writing a report have remained useful throughout my career. I could not get rid of the feeling that our micro strategy of analyzing case details was missing a macro component, the role of the state and its policies (or lack thereof). Much later when I analyzed the flourishing of NGOs in Bangladesh, I realized how they burgeoned in the absence of government. I feel fortunate to have witnessed the beginnings of social change from the front lines.

I started flirting with the idea of an academic job, a career I had decided never to pursue having grown up as a child of two academics, because the lure of flexibility and freedom was impossible to resist in the middle of a hectic career with long hours and long commutes. I tried my luck at Shahjalal University in Sylhet, especially as my friend Noyon, who was teaching there, kept telling me what fun he was having. The interview went well, and my husband and I made a mini-vacation of it by taking the night train to Sylhet. The interview pool was impressive, but the candidate who got the job was the least impressive one. University jobs, like other jobs, required knowing the right people and having the influence to pull strings. An academic job would have made my pursuit of higher education much easier. But I decided to forego that route to try to get admission in universities abroad on my own.

I had taken the TOEFL earlier and it was still valid. The TOEFL was managed by the British Council, which I always thought of as an extension of my home. Compared to the TOEFL, I found the GRE more demanding; creating the time to study was a challenge. When I was not in Matlab I stayed late in my office after everyone left to prepare for the GRE, especially the math section. Math was actually the easiest part, but the difficulty lay in the fact that I had never done math in English. I had to translate the terminology before I got to the math itself. I loved the analytical section. The vocabulary part was difficult but not without fun. Because of the time crunch, I was reduced to memorizing most of the words, which I tried to do everywhere, in the bus on my way to the office, in the middle of housework, cooking, anywhere I thought of it. I had bought a deck of cards, an accessory to the GRE book, which I carried everywhere.

Maria, the American student from Maryland who was working as an intern, was preparing for medical school. Often we ended up in the empty office studying together. She was my source of information on American schools. I asked her to test me on my vocabulary and she in turn asked me to help her with her Bangla. Maria's confusions about Bangladeshi society and the funny incidents that arose from unintended meanings entertained us to no end. Listening to her mix-ups about Bangla was an eye-opener. The exceptions seemed to dominate the rules of grammar. We have two different words for "half," applicable to things or time. The mistakes were understandable as the cues stem not from logic but intuition. Later in life, explaining the logic of Bangla grammar to my non-Bengali husband proved even more disastrous as he tried to apply the rules of Urdu and Gujarati.

ICDDR,B opened an email account and in those days there was a generic address for everyone working at ICDDR,B, which meant that the person using the only computer assigned for emails got to read everyone's messages. Maria and her boyfriend in America were exchanging emails and she tried to be the first one on the computer to preempt anyone else from reading her boyfriend's messages. I remember sitting with her and sending my first email to my sister who was already studying in America. Maria was fond of wearing saree and wore it more often than I did in the office. For my mother's generation, after their mid-teens the saree was the only acceptable dress outside private quarters. For us, the dress code had expanded to include shalwar kameez and certain Western attire, depending on the occasion and place. Wearing shalwar kameez was easier than donning the unstitched eleven-yard-long fabric wrapped around a skirt-like petticoat and a tight-fitting blouse. Perhaps no other dress in the world accommodates the wearer's individual sense of style as flexibly as the saree. It can be worn very modestly or revealingly with every possible variation during the course of the day without commitment to any particular way of self-presentation. The choice of accessories and the way of wearing them make the same saree easily adaptable to different occasions. The saree for me demanded an occasion, something to celebrate, even if it was only having a good day. Maria, on the other hand, wore the saree indiscriminately, buying her own, borrowing, or swapping with her hired help. This last action was a social fiasco because of unwritten rules. Her lack of consciousness of social norms and taboos generated not only laughter, but a lot of self-questioning for me.

The political situation was getting volatile again. Hartal after hartal piled on. At first, hartal days provided the opportunity to stay home and rest. But soon, our employer figured out a way to make up for lost hours by asking us to show up after the hartal was over and on holidays. At the time, we had frequent half-day hartals. So we went to the office at noon and returned at eight p.m. As political conflict gained momentum, hartals became all-day affairs and we had to give up holidays to work. We got the hartal days off, but it was useless because we could not go out. Hartal norms have relaxed in recent decades, allowing rickshaws to operate, but back then, unless there was an emergency, no one dared to go out and risk the wrath of the opposition. B brought his work home, though often he opted to stay at his office the night before the hartal. One of his partners had a car in which B picked me up from my office. While it was exhilarating to zoom past jammed traffic in a car instead of a bus, the magic of riding on the back of his motorcycle, holding on to him tightly, managing my flying hair and dupatta at the same time, and fearing the watchful eyes of relatives and neighbors who seemed to be present everywhere at all hours, was never again resurrected.

At last I was determined to apply to foreign schools for my master's. After the TOEFL, the next hurdle was the GRE. It was not only the question of taking the tests, but knowing where and how to apply. My lifelong exposure to the British Council proved irrelevant as it was only the library at the American embassy which held the secrets of going abroad. Unlike the British Council library, which in my mind remained associated with non-academic and cultural pursuits, the library at the American embassy was businesslike in character. I was only admitted to the wing which held a collection of bulky volumes of Barron's guides to various schools and to the TOEFL and the GRE, but

I never saw the rest of the library which was located near the commercial center of the city, crowded and busy. My connections with the American embassy remained sparse, limited to getting information to apply to American universities. We were given an hour's time to sift through the imposing manuals. When the hour was over, the librarian told us to come back the next day, which was not very helpful, since I had to take leave from my office and spend considerable time commuting. The American embassy, even in the pre-9/11 days, was never welcoming and never upheld any of the principles of openness, equality, or even basic decency in their encounters with the native population.

I had to decide which school I would apply to, since I could send the scores to five schools for free. At the time I hadn't heard the term Russian roulette, but that was how I decided my future. With little guidance, I thought that applying everywhere—America, Canada, Australia—would maximize my chances. I applied to Australian universities first as their sessions started in March rather than September. I was accepted to two universities, both without any financial aid. One was the Australian National University, another was Monash University, where I had applied solely on a whim, being impressed by pictures of the campus. Someone told me that the campus was windy and in the weeks between my acceptance and withdrawal I would daydream about standing in a barren landscape, wind blowing my hair and clothes. The only way for me to attend any program abroad was some scholarship or work opportunity to cover my tuition and boarding. I had saved enough money to pay for my passage, but my dream was unattainable without a scholarship.

We could buy the preparation guides to the TOEFL and the GRE in any bookstore; even the footpath booksellers had them, usually the cheap Indian prints. But the American embassy library had all the guides to colleges in the U.S. which were available nowhere else. The internet already existed in 1994, the year of my preparation, but it did not exist for me. I had only limited time to sift through the voluminous reference books, but there were so many universities. How did one make up one's mind? Was there any formula for choosing one's college? Not only did I not have any particular regional preference, but my knowledge of geographic diversity was shamefully inadequate. I knew of the Ivy League colleges and knew that I shouldn't waste time applying to the very best places. Had I done the right research, I would have learned that the very best places are often interested in the issues I had expertise in. In the end, I chose several universities, some based on name recognition, some because I took a liking to something—the name or pictures or fleeting intuition (which failed miserably). Armed with a cartload of random information, which I did not know how to sift through, I started my application process. At the last moment, I thought it would be helpful to throw a Canadian university into the mix. My friend Miti handed me an application package from a Canadian university she had asked for in the mail but had decided not to use. When I applied to Dalhousie University, not only had I never heard of it, but Nova Scotia was also an unknown entity to me. I would discover that my sense of geography about Canada was pitiful. I got admitted to several places, but Dalhousie University was the only one which offered a full scholarship, making my decision easy in the end. I remember having to explain to everyone where

Nova Scotia was, and everyone kept saying, oh, it is the one on the other side. Halifax could never compete with Vancouver, even before the latter's economic boom. When I eventually got my job at Texas A&M International University in Laredo, Texas, it was yet another geographic challenge to explain where I was going. I had to look at the map to figure out for myself where Laredo was when I was applying. It is ironic that geography shapes so much of our destiny, whom we meet and how we live our lives, yet in school I thought of geography only as a means to daydream and found it difficult to draw maps.

I started getting letters of acceptance by the late spring of 1995. Although each letter boosted my morale and filled me with joy, without a scholarship or graduate assistantship their offers remained unattainable for me. A few universities did mention the possibility of a graduate assistantship, especially after the first semester if my grades were good, but even one semester's tuition was beyond my means. All I had was the money I had saved from my salary, only enough to pay for my ticket. At the time, the dollar was worth thirty times the taka. I was sick and tired of multiplying by thirty and figuring out the huge amount of taka I needed to amass to realize my dreams. After a few agonizing months, in mid-summer I got the acceptance letter from Dalhousie University along with the offer of a scholarship. The scholarship would pay for my tuition and most of my costs. I was in seventh heaven. But I had to descend to earth rather quickly as it would take three months to get the Canadian visa, and by that time, classes would have started. Someone in the office knew a person who worked in the Canadian embassy. He advised me to finish my medical exams and get all the paperwork ready. Although the interview for the visa was scheduled three months later, he snuck me in when a Canadian immigration officer was visiting the Dhaka office for some other purpose. Everything went well and I also got an American visa to stop on my way and see my sister, friends, and uncles for two weeks before classes started.

The process of getting visas to America and Canada defied all logic. It seemed designed to instill feelings of hopelessness and being at the total mercy of immigration officers, stripping the applicant of any shred of dignity. We heard how everything was smooth and easy once you landed in America or Canada, and it really was, right after customs, as soon as you entered the land. Why on earth was it so complicated, illogical, and bureaucratic at the consulates in Dhaka? If an embassy is a reflection of a country, both the Canadian and the American embassies, especially the latter, projected images of their countries far removed from the pleasant, friendly, and freedom-loving self-image they touted. People had to languish outside the embassies, in open space, come rain or shine, for hours and hours. The wait alone, standing on one's feet for four to six hours, was a gauntlet to anyone, especially the elderly and sick. I understand that the officers were weeding out those who should be denied visas (incidentally, my experiences were all pre-9/11), but the lack of politeness and basic decency toward most people was unpardonable. Rather than being ambassadors of goodwill, they portrayed a high-handedness that seemed to scream that you, the applicant from a poor country, would forever depend on their indulgence.

Leaving my job was painful. I had a tacit understanding with my boss that if I wanted to return after my degree, he would find a place for me at ICDDR,B. Had I worked for a few more years, I would have had a realistic chance of being selected for the exchange program at Harvard. I was tempted to do so, and to this day I wonder how my life would have been different had I chosen that option. But I had already put changes into motion and I did not want to stall anymore. I knew it was time to leave. The day I bought the plane ticket, I took out all my savings to pay the travel agent. I can still see the travel agent counting the money as I stared at the ticket and wondered if I was doing the right thing. The final few weeks went by dizzyingly. There was so much to do. So many people to see and say goodbye to, the nervous thrill of shopping, the paperwork that sucked up time.

Between the office and unending errands, shopping, and visits to friends and family to bid farewell, I avoided thinking about what it meant for me and my marriage to leave my husband behind in Dhaka. While Bangladesh sends a disproportionately high number of expatriates working abroad, the cultural stigma of being a male who was left behind was present in our case. B's partner's wife had left for higher studies, never to return, and they had recently finalized their divorce. The easy way out was not to talk about these issues, which is what we did. Although I had every intention of returning after my master's, I knew that the two-year stint in Canada would change my life forever.

My last days in Dhaka went by in a blur. I was relieved to be pulled into all kinds of activities, some practical, some social, which gave me little time to reflect. One of my last fond memories is of the boat ride at Parjatan restaurant in Uttara, where B invited my cousins, Zafreen and Farzana, without telling me and surprised me. It was a restaurant near the airport which we always passed on our way home and I had wondered about the small pond and the boats I could see from afar. One of my saddest memories is of leaving Shucheta, whom I had promised to bring back a life-sized doll, a promise I never kept, which still rankles me.

I remember buying a lot of clothes from Bangabazar, discarded or redundant clothes that failed to make it to Walmart or other U.S. stores and were invariably out of style in Canada. Stylish or not, they were lifesavers. My maroon five hundred taka (less than ten dollars) winter jacket was worth seventy or eighty dollars in North America. My clothes, some books, and gifts made my suitcases heavy as lead. I did not even have a Pullman. Armed with the huge suitcases, lugging the inconvenient hand baggage, I started a new chapter in my story. The day I left was a half-day hartal. My parents came after the hartal was over and stayed until my flight in the evening. The goodbye congregation at the airport followed the Bengali tradition of too many people, too many teary eyes, and too much advice.

Between packing and spending time with the rest of the family, B and I had little time to ourselves. When we did, we both knew we stood at a threshold and wanted to avoid dealing with the reality as long as possible. We still made plans about how I would look for master's programs in architecture near my campus so he could come and be with me for at least a year before we both came back to Dhaka. This half-heartedly concocted plan was just enough to keep our hopes for the marriage alive. We were both more tender and forgiving in the last few weeks, which again made us feel that we could work out our differences. We both knew that my departure would be the point of no return, yet we did not want to confront the truth. At the very last moment at the airport, B paid extra money to gain permission to come inside with me, and suddenly he said, "I am not going to see you ever again!"